SLOTS CONQUEST

How to Beat the Slot Machines!

Frank Scoblete

TRIUMPH
B O O K S

Triumph Books and colophon are registered trademarks of Random House, Inc.

Library of Congress Cataloging-in-Publication Data

Scoblete, Frank.
  Slots conquest : how to beat the slot machines! / Frank Scoblete.
     p. cm.
  ISBN-13: 978-1-60078-335-7
  ISBN-10: 1-60078-335-X
  1. Slot machines. 2. Gambling. I. Title.
  GV1311.S56S37 2010
  795.2'7—dc22

                              2010036183

This book is available in quantity at special discounts for your group or organization. For further information, contact:

Triumph Books
542 South Dearborn Street
Suite 750
Chicago, Illinois 60605
(312) 939-3330
Fax (312) 663-3557
www.triumphbooks.com

Printed in U.S.A.
ISBN: 978-1-60078-335-7
Design by Patricia Frey

To Jerry "Stickman"

Contents

Author's Note: *At times I am going to interchange the words "coins" and "credits" because today some slot players think in terms of credits on the machine and some slot players still think of those credits as coins or dollars. I will also talk about money too because ultimately that is what it is all about.*

CHAPTER 1

Those Wonderful
One-Armed Bandits

More people enjoy casino gambling than go bowling. More adult Americans go to casinos than go to Major League Baseball games. Casino gambling is more popular than tennis, football, soccer, boxing, and professional wrestling. There are more casino gamblers than there are viewers for the top-rated television shows. I'm guessing there are more casino gamblers in America than there are adults having sex tonight.

Most Americans now live within 300 miles of a casino, so enjoying a day, a night, or a few days or nights of casino fun is not out of the norm for America's approximately 54 million casino players. It used to be that going to Vegas or illegal joints were the only ways to get your gambling juices boiling, but now, with casinos in a majority of the states, players spending time in Lady Luck's cathedrals is not unusual. And we love to spend time in the casinos. I'm certain that readers of this book are avid casino players.

Casino gambling is a multibillion-dollar industry. The cash cow, the golden goose, and the treasure chest of this industry is the once-lowly slot machine. Strangely enough, it wasn't until 1984 that slot machines made more money for Atlantic City and Las Vegas casinos than did the table games. Until that time casinos were associated with table games, not slot machines. The top table game until about 1963 was craps; after 1963 it was blackjack. Roulette always had a following as "the third

1

game," and those carnival games you now see spread throughout the table-game areas, such as Let It Ride, Three-Card Poker, and Caribbean Stud (plus many more!) didn't come into the houses of chance until after the slot machines made their move to take over the casino world.

In those heady pre-1984 days—especially from 1942 through 1978, with the opening of Atlantic City—the slot machines were considered the province of women. Cigar-smoking middle-aged craps players wearing impeccable suits could be heard saying, "Hey, baby, here's some change. Go play the machines." That was then.

This is now: About 80 percent of all women casino-goers play the slot machines, while about 63 percent of the men do so. The table games are still dominated by men, with craps having about a 90 percent male majority and blackjack and roulette seeing smaller male majorities but majorities nevertheless.

Obviously surveys show that women like playing the machines, and many of the machines are geared to this female clientele. Note the number of new machines each year that have movie titles, television titles, or star titles as their branding. Most of these machines are clearly aimed at women—although many machines are geared toward a male demographic as well (the Star Wars and comic-book machines, for example).

Why women prefer slots to table games in such a huge majority is not truly known with certainty. Maybe the tables seem more competitive, combative, and judgmental. After all, rarely does anyone tell you how to play the slots, but many blackjack "experts" do not hesitate to tell other blackjack players how to play their hands or scold them if they just played a hand incorrectly. Whether the blackjack "expert" actually knows how to play is irrelevant—he *thinks* he knows how to play, and that is enough for him to lambaste anyone who plays differently.

But those 63 percent of males playing those machines is where the cosmic increase in slot play has occurred. The men of the old days rarely played slot machines, and, if they did, they played a few coins here or there, nothing major.

Once men broke into slot play in large numbers at the same time that casinos were spreading like wildfire throughout the country, the die was cast—or rather the RNG was twirled—and slot machines became the *big* thing.

The slot-machine aficionado is not only the preferred player in the casinos but a player many casino advertisers wish to reach. Look at casinos' television commercials, and they feature slot players more than table-game players, a thing unheard of before 1985. Can you imagine James Bond playing a Betty Boop machine?

Slot machines are no longer chump change to the casinos. Using average paybacks released by casino jurisdictions for various denominations, with a 12-spin-per-minute play rate and three coins being played, a 25¢ slot player's expectation is to lose about $54 per hour based on a house edge of 10 percent. A $1 slot player's expectation is to lose about $194 per hour, based on a house edge of 9 percent. A $5 slot player's expectation is to lose about $432 per hour, based on a house edge of 4 percent.

Compare the slot figures with the following table games: At blackjack, playing about 80 hands per hour, a $25 basic-strategy player is expected to lose about $10 to $25 per hour; a $50 player between $20 and $50 per hour; and a $100 blackjack player between $40 and $100 per hour. A baccarat player making a combination of Bank and Player bets, playing 50 decisions per hour at $100 per hand, will be expected to lose between $60 and $70 per hour. A roulette player, playing 50 spins per hour, with a $25 average bet, is expected to lose about $66 per hour.

The casinos understand this completely. A $1 slot player makes more money for the casino than a $100 baccarat player, because unlike the table games, the machines don't need to work eight-hour shifts, get into arguments with floor personnel, receive medical benefits, get sick days and vacation days, or have mood swings. Slot machines are cheap employees with rich people's returns for the casinos' minor investments. They cost the casino far less than table games.

And each year machines that aren't working as well as other machines or that don't seem to have the potential player interest of newer models coming off the line can be replaced without those awkward words: "Sorry, John, you're fired!" Slot machines are relatively headache-free, as are slot players.

Casinos don't even have to worry about advantage slot players taking their money, even when some progressive machines get into positive territory. You will learn about such machines in this book. That is correct, you can become an advantage slot player (or close to it) if you follow the advice I'll give you in these pages. Even with you winning money from the positive machines, it is still no big deal to the casinos because the machine is making the programmed amount of money for the casino over time despite occasionally being in a player-positive mode. If you are savvy and only play the advantage-play machines when they are in a positive mode, you could be a long-term winner at these specific slots. Not a bad situation at all.

There are many benefits to slot play for the player too. You don't get game interference at the slot machines. Most other slot players don't care whether you play one coin, two coins, three coins, or fifty coins or whether you are superstitious or happy or depressed or clinically insane. Most slot players exist in a world of their own; they are cocooned and only occasionally interrupted by the screams of some other slot player who has just won a big one and can't keep from yelling her good fortune to the world. Slot players rejoice when other slot players win and then quickly go back to doing what they love to do—playing those machines.

While slot play is overwhelmingly the game of choice for both women and men, savvy slot aficionados recognize an interesting peculiarity in their slot-playing brethren. Slot players lose interest in all types of machines relatively quickly. They will play a given machine for a period of time and then abandon it. One slot player said, "I loved the Elvis machines, but I never won on them, so I quit playing them and moved on to Betty Boop machines." And what happened? "I didn't have much better luck on Betty, so I dumped her too."

Like bad marriages, slot players and slot machines divorce rather often. Slot players are the Henry VIIIs of casino gamers—always looking for the perfect match to have monetary offspring and never finding it. This is probably due to the fact that most slot players lose most of the time on all the machines. By switching machines so frequently, they hope to switch their luck. Unfortunately, the machines are not programmed to increase the players' luck. They are programmed to increase the casinos' bucks.

Casino executives know of the brittle relationship of slot player to slot machine, and that's why each and every year you will note how many new machines make their way onto the casino floors. All casino gaming shows, such as G2E (Global Gaming Expo), are dominated by new machines. There may be no difference in payouts between Betty Boop machines and Shirley Temple machines, but they look different and sound different, and the slot player will jump from one to the other hoping they are actually different.

The first law of slot machines is "keep them coming," because new machines will be tried by players. You will not see this same jumping around at table games. Craps players don't abandon their favorite game because, whether they win or lose, they love the game of craps. Blackjack players are loyal as well. You will not see many new table games at gaming shows and, while some new table games have gotten a foothold in the casinos, compared to the number of new machines out there, the number of new table games is infinitesimal.

Still, the paybacks on slot machines make them tough sells. Most have edges over 5 percent (a loss of $5 for every $100 wagered), many have edges over 10 percent (a loss of $10 for every $100 wagered), and some have edges of over 15 percent (a loss of $15 for every $100 wagered). These are big edges to monstrous edges, and when combined with the high speeds with which slot players attack the machines, they add up to frequent and often large losses. Very few people will stay in a marriage where they are abused, and slot players don't want to stay at machines that have been cuffing them around for any period of time. So on to the new machines they go with hope burning in their hearts. Slot players are like a country song called "I Keep Losing My Love, but I Never Give Up!"

Of course, if slot payouts were really generous, say 99.5 percent (the casino having a ½ percent edge in that case—which is the approximate house edge against a basic-strategy player at blackjack), then the chance is fairly good that the slot player would stick with such a machine come hell, high water, or new slot inventories. Getting some kind of return on a gambling investment is the best way for casinos to keep their players playing. The second-best way is to offer new machines. The casinos prefer to offer new machines.

There is really no end in sight to the slot revolution that has taken place in the casinos. In 1984, in both Atlantic City and Las Vegas, the slots made more money than the table games for the first time, and their growth since then has been nothing short of phenomenal. While 50 percent of all marriages end in divorce, most divorced people still want to get remarried. And slot players still want to play the machines even after they have divorced numerous previous machines. It's the way of the slot world.

CHAPTER 2

The RNG, the Paybacks, and the Hit Frequency

Throw a projectile into a giant room crammed with tens of thousands of Ping-Pong balls sitting atop mousetraps (or some kind of propelling agent), and when that projectile hits some of those Ping-Pong balls on those mousetraps, all hell breaks loose. Ping-Pong balls rocket all over the place, causing other balls to rocket all over the place, hitting other balls on the mousetraps and in the air too. Before you know it, the room looks like Alaska in a snowstorm, with Ping-Pong balls flying, hitting, and bouncing all over the place. There is no way to predict what balls will hit what other balls. It's a random distribution, unpredictable in practice and fast as all get out.

And that is like the RNG—or random number generator, or Really Nifty Gadget—that decides what symbols will appear on the face of the machine you are playing. It determines these symbols by creating sequences of random numbers, perhaps thousands of sequences, so that when the play button is pressed or the handle is pulled, the RNG tells the reels (or video segments) what should show up. The RNG is contained in a computer chip, and this chip will determine everything that goes on with the machine's selections. The job of the player is simple in this scheme of things: she merely tells the machine to tell her what symbols the RNG just selected for her. She does this by pressing the play button.

The RNG is functioning all the time, even when the machine is not being played (some RNGs might pause when the machine is not being played, but this is unusual), so that when one hits the play button, the RNG will immediately shoot out the symbols for the slot player to see. But that RNG sequence and associated symbols would not have been had the slot player pressed the play button a second later or a second earlier.

Knowing this, you can see that certain slot myths such as "You stole my jackpot!" can't be true. No play button can be hit at the exact same time. If your dastardly competitor pushes your hand out of the way to press the play button, the sequence of symbols is not the same as the sequence you would have gotten, owing to the slight pause between pushing your hand away and then pressing the button. Yes, it is that fast. So if your competitor wins the jackpot, you probably would not have won it had you pressed that button.

Payback Percentages

You might have seen advertisements in some casino venues stating that their machines return 98 percent of the money played. The casinos make such a payback look as if it is a great thing. In reality, what the casino is saying is actually, "You put in $100, and we'll give you back $98." Of course, this is the expected value over time—a $2 loss for every $100 played. Naturally, the first $100 you put in might win you thousands or lose you every penny. But over time the expected value in real life will be the expected value programmed into the machine. There's no escaping it—reel life and real life ultimately even out. Given the number of machines the casinos have and the number of decisions those machines give out, the casinos are on top in a very short period of time—and the money just rolls in.

So how is the machine going to pay out this money? How does it know to keep $2 per $100 wagered? If we take a strictly random coin toss of heads and tails, the odds are 50/50 that you'll hit whatever side of the coin on which you are betting. In a fair game where the casino has no edge and you have no edge, a $100 bet will win you $100 or lose you $100. Over enough time the expectation is for you and the casino to be even.

But what if the casino decides to pay you $96 for your wins but still take the $100 from you when you lose? Well, the casino now has a

2 percent edge over you. For $100 wagered, you win one ($96) and lose one ($100), so the $200 you bet returns you $196—a 98 percent return on the money you played. The casino is now keeping $2 per every $100 you wager.

Obviously inside that slot machine's payback programming are thousands of combinations appearing and disappearing constantly, but all of them *combined* follow the basic concept of a random coin toss, where the casino will pay back less than it takes in. That's how the casino makes its profit.

There is no way to change this, short of taking a sledgehammer to the machine and walloping it, which means over time slot players must lose. Even advantage-play machines (which you will read about in Chapter 24) win money for the casinos because the machine is only in a player-favorable mode for a small percentage of the time. The rest of the time, the house has its nice fat edge. That's why advantage slot players must only play these machines at those times when the machine is in that positive mode. To do otherwise is to be playing a losing game.

How do the casinos know that the programming will work itself out? Go back to the coin toss. Heads and tails will each appear half the time. The casino cannot lose when that machine is played over an extended period of time. And don't just think of one machine of a 50/50 coin toss that short-changes on the wins; think of hundreds of thousands of them, each churning out decisions every few seconds. The casino is in the long run in a rather short period of time due to the total number of machines slot players are playing. The casinos *must* win, and they certainly *do* win—*a lot*.

The same principle applies to the linked-progressive machines. The linked machines either each have an individual RNG that will signal the main jackpot computer that the jackpot line has been hit, or all the machines are being run by a central RNG. In reality, it does not matter how the machines are set up; the paybacks will follow the programming in terms of what the casino gives and what the casino takes—and naturally what the casino takes will far outweigh what it gives.

What Pays What

Over time there has been little change in the actual payback percentages on the various denominations of traditional machines. The traditional penny machines return about 85 percent, nickel machines return about 88 percent, the 25¢ machines return about 90 percent, the 50¢ machines return a little over 90 percent, the $1 machines return about 91 to 92 percent, and the $5 machines return about 94 to 95 percent.

Some venues are more generous than others. The Las Vegas Strip machines are tighter than the off-Strip casinos, which cater to Las Vegas locals. Tunica in Mississippi is more generous than Atlantic City. But the averages throughout the United States and Canada still tend to hover around the percentages I gave above.

If you read magazines that give the payback percentages of a casino's machines and note some really high or low returns on $5, $10, $50, and $100 machines, this is caused by the fact that there are not as many of these machines in the casino, and thus the total amount of play is not as large as play on the 25¢ and $1 machines. The casino needs the long run for the percentages to work themselves out. The number of decisions is the key variable for the casinos. The more decisions the machine spews, the better—for the casino—and the worse for the player.

Now, with the *new* penny and nickel machines, the ones that give you the chance to play 50 to 100 coins, you are not getting a good deal—you are in fact getting a rotten deal. You might be putting in $2.50 to $5 in nickels, but that $5 is not being paid at the normal $5 rate; nor is your $2.50 getting a normal dollar's payback percentage. These machines are money gobblers, as most just pay back the very low traditional penny and nickel percentages. The normal $5 machine will be paying 94–95 percent, but the $5 you put in the nickel models will be paying back about 88 percent—a radically worse return.

My advice is to skip playing these machines. You are not getting any kind of bargain on them, so dump them from your playing plan. If you play them, you will no longer be a low-level player but a much higher one who is foolishly giving the casino a much bigger edge on a lot more money.

Hit Frequency

Not all slot-machine decisions return money to the player. In fact, most slot players have been trained to expect long stretches of play without any returns at all. A return on a slot machine is called a "hit," as in "I didn't hit anything" or "I was hitting like crazy all night."

The hit frequency is how often a player gets some kind of a *return*. It is not, as some would think, how often a player wins. A return of two coins for three coins played is considered a hit, but it is obviously not a win.

Most slot machines have hit frequencies between 9 percent and about 25 percent, which means that a player will get a hit, on average, 9–25 times out of 100 spins. Some of these hits will be for marginal returns, and fewer will be for decent or big wins.

In an informal study of slot players, I discovered that a slight majority want to be in on bigger hits, meaning bigger wins, instead of having frequent hits, and therefore they tend to prefer machines with lower hit frequencies but bigger payouts. I had thought it would be just the opposite, steady hits and less waiting time instead of infrequent larger hits with much longer waiting times. The reality did not correspond to my intuition.

CHAPTER 3

Which Machines to Play and Which to Avoid

ost slot players want to know which machines they should play to get the best return on their money, usually termed "loose machines," and which machines they should avoid, usually termed "tight machines." Of course, some slot players don't care about loose or tight machines because they have one focus and one focus only: to play machines such as Megabucks that can change their lives in dramatic ways. Winning millions is their dream.

While the terms "loose" and "tight" are relative—some casinos' loose machines could be some other casinos' tight machines—there are some absolutes that one can garner from slot-machine payback statistics. The hierarchy of machines, from estimated lowest returns to highest returns, is as follows:

Machine Denomination	Estimated Return	House Edge	Expected Loss
Penny Machines	83–88 percent	17–12 percent	$17–$12 per $100
Nickel Machines	88 percent	12 percent	$12 per $100
10¢ Machines	88 percent	12 percent	$12 per $100
25¢ Machines	90 percent	10 percent	$10 per $100
50¢ Machines	90 percent	10 percent	$10 per $100

Machine Denomination	Estimated Return	House Edge	Expected Loss
$1 Machines	92 percent	8 percent	$8 per $100
$5 Machines	94–95 percent	6–5 percent	$6–$5 per $100
$10+ Machines	96–98 percent	4–2 percent	$4–$2 per $100

Obviously the casinos make far more money on their higher-denomination machines even though the casinos are more "generous" with the returns on such machines. A smaller percentage of a lot more money makes the casinos a lot more money.

Not all machines in all denominations return the above averages. Progressive machines are tighter than nonprogressive machines on all denominations, and linked progressives are tighter still. For example, the abovementioned $1 Megabucks machine probably has a house edge of between 12 and 15 percent (give or take a little) because it needs to bring in enough money to pay off the giant jackpots it offers and for the casinos to pay for the licensing of these machines. So your expectation on Megabucks is pretty poor in the slot-machine scheme of things.

Stand-alone machines that are not progressive will be looser because they do not have to generate an escalating jackpot. Stand-alone machines that offer no reward for multiple coins played are far better than progressive machines. Such machines might offer a $400 jackpot on one coin, an $800 jackpot for two coins, and a $1,200 jackpot for three coins (or a $1,199 jackpot to avoid paying taxes). Note that you get absolutely no benefit from playing extra coins. A three-coin player is merely tripling his losses per spin.

Advantage-play machines are in a somewhat different category. Their overall return will not be much different from the hierarchy above, but at certain times these machines enter a positive territory—positive for the player, that is—and positive if the player knows what to look for and how to play the machine when it is in the positive mode. This fact does not change the machine's overall return to the casino. The casino has the edge on these machines over the players who play them when they are both negative and positive. What the advantage-slot player wants to do is never play them in a negative mode. Let the other slot players waste their money when the machines are in a negative mode.

So how should you play the variety of slot machines crammed into our modern casinos? (I'll handle the advantage machines in Chapters 24 and 25.)

The Full or Maximum-Coins Dilemma

"Always play maximum coins," say the wags of the slot-machine world. After all, they'll say, if you play one coin, the jackpot returns $400; and if you play two coins, the machine returns $800; but if you play three coins, the return on the jackpot is $1,600. That third coin gives you more money on the jackpot.

Sounds good and true, but looked at more closely, putting three coins in the machine actually costs you *much* more money per session and in your slot playing career than just playing one coin.

Without going into arcane math, it is simple to see why playing full coin even on machines that reward full coin on their jackpots is a massive waste of your money. Your chances of hitting the jackpot might be 5,000-to-1 (it might also be more or less). If you play long enough you will probably hit that jackpot, perhaps many times in your slot-playing career. Your reward for playing those extra two coins is a mere $400.

Given a normal session of two hours of play on a $1 machine, playing 12 spins per minute, you will play 1,440 decisions per two-hour session. Now check out the play record of two individuals, one playing one coin and one playing three (maximum) coins using our $400, $800, and $1,600 jackpot lines, and see why the "always play full coin" bromide will actually make your bankroll convulse.

Okay, let me speculate that the return on the machine when you play one coin is 90 percent (a loss of $10 per $100 wagered) and the return on full coin is 90.5—a full ½ percent better because of the extra money on the jackpot line. So the 90.5 percent includes the hitting of the jackpot—keep that in mind. The jackpot is not extra. Each line is a two-hour session.

1 Coin Per 2 hours of Play	Expected Loss Per 2 Hours	Expected 10 Session Loss	Full Coin Per 2 Hours of Play	Expected Loss Per 2 Hours	Expected 10 Session Loss
$1,440	$144	$144	$4,320	$410.40	$410.40
$1,440	$144	$288	$4,320	$410.40	$820.80
$1,440	$144	$432	$4,320	$410.40	$1,231.20
$1,440	$144	$576	$4,320	$410.40	$1,641.60
$1,440	$144	$720	$4,320	$410.40	$2,052
$1,440	$144	$864	$4,320	$410.40	$2,462.40
$1,440	$144	$1,008	$4,320	$410.40	$2,872.80
$1,440	$144	$1,152	$4,320	$410.40	$3,283.20
$1,440	$144	$1,296	$4,320	$410.40	$3,693.60
$1,440	$144	$1,440	$4,320	$410.40	$4,104
Total	----------	$1,440 loss	----------	----------	$4,104 loss

The comparative losses between the two styles of play are nothing short of staggering. The maximum-coin player is expected to lose $2,664 more than the one-coin player in 10 sessions. Now push such play forward in time—100 sessions, 1,000 sessions—and you can see how awful the losses will be for the person betting maximum coin. So even though the machine returns $400 more on the jackpot, this does not really help the player in terms of time played and money lost at the machines. This holds true for every denomination of machine as well—maximum coin costs you a lot more money. It's an inarguable fact of slot-playing life.

So play one coin, unless losing more money makes you excited, in which case you probably need a good psychiatrist and not a slot machine.

Obviously on machines where there is no reward for playing maximum coin (such as $400, $800, and $1,200), you just play one coin. Do not waste your money by tripling your play. It makes no sense to do such a thing. These machines are called "Equal Distribution Machines." They are the best to play in the stand-alone category.

"Buy a Pay" or "Buy a Play" Machines

Are there any machines where you are better off playing maximum coins? Yes, in fact there are—although traditional ones are not as widespread as they once were. These are called "Buy a Pay" or "Buy a Play" machines. These machines offer you more winning pay lines with the more coins you play. The house edge gets slightly lower on the second coin, but it plummets when you play three coins, which opens up all sorts of winning lines.

These machines do call for you to play maximum coin because they are returning a much, much higher percentage on such play. However (isn't there always a "however"?), you really should slow down your play on these machines since you are still betting three times as much money, and bad streaks can really cripple you. Slow and easy is the way to go—in fact, it's the way to go on all slot machines except for the advantage-play ones I'll be discussing in Chapter 24.

Certified Machines

Some casinos like to lure their players with signs that say their machines in this particular bank are certified to return a certain percentage of the money played in them—usually 97 or 98 percent. If the signage says "All the Machines," then you can be confident that each and every machine in this bank will have the same payback percentage. If the sign says something to the effect that "Our Machines Pay Up to 98 Percent," then that means only some—*or one*—machine(s) in the bank will pay back that amount. The rest could be as tight as pre-ghost-visit Scrooge. "Up to" is the key wording in the bad certified machines.

Obviously it is always best to play machines guaranteeing such high returns, yet you will see ploppy players pass these by as if such certification is irrelevant. I've seen people playing those monster linked progressives that come in with house edges around 15 percent right next to the bank of certified machines where "all" the machines are returning 98 percent.

Those New Penny and Nickel Machines Can Kill You

You think of yourself as a low-roller, and you prefer to play penny and nickel slot machines so you don't lose too much money, but you are getting your butt kicked big time! Yes, you must play full coin to get all the lines to give you the maximum wins that you long for. How many lines? Some machines are floating around where you can play 100 credits! On a penny machine you would be betting $1 per spin. On a nickel machine you would be betting $5 per spin. Welcome to the high-roller section of slot play, Mr., Mrs., Miss, or Ms.!

Not only are you now betting with the big boys and big girls, but the casino is truly milking you like a farmer milking a slow-witted cow because those penny and nickel machines have the worst payback percentages in the casinos. Yes, these paybacks are far, far worse than the traditional $1 and $5 machines. The casino has suckered you into playing a lot more money with a much bigger house edge.

Obviously, if you think of yourself as a low-roller, then make sure you play *one penny* or *one nickel*, but leave it at that amount even if it takes the strongest willpower you have ever displayed in your life. If you want to play 25 pennies, move up to a 25¢ machine; the same holds true for nickels. Want to play five nickels? Go to the quarter machines. Don't throw your money down a toilet, which is exactly what you will be doing if you play these new penny and nickel monsters for more than just a single penny or nickel.

Check out this chart and see what a horror show those low-roller machines can be. Each column will show the expected loss based on a return percentage of 85 for penny machines and 88 for nickel machines. The quarter machines will return 90 percent, and the $1 machines will return 92 percent. We'll do 1,440 spins for a two-hour session.

Penny Machine 25 Credits (25¢)	Penny Machine 100 Credits ($1.00)	Nickel Machine 5 Credits (25¢)	Nickel Machine 20 Credits ($1.00)	Quarter Machine One Coin (25¢)	Dollar Machine One Coin ($1.00)
$50	$200	$43.20	$172.80	$36	115.20

You can see that moving up to the traditional machines is a far better way to play than to remain on these money-hungry mega-multiline monsters. True, these megamultiline penny and nickel machines have excellent cartoons and drawings and music, but, come on, watching some hobgoblin dancing around is not as much fun as saving your money from its ravenous, hungry, insatiable dripping jaws.

This Machine Is *Hot*!

A brilliant slot executive—and I mean *brilliant* with no sarcasm—came up with an in-house advertising plan that really sent people scurrying to play certain machines. He or she put signs on perhaps 10 to 20 percent of a given casino's slot inventory that said, "This machine is HOT!" if the machine had hit a jackpot or several large payouts in the past week.

If a machine had been ice cold the previous week, the sign read: "This machine is DUE!" Depending on a slot player's sense of trending, the player either went *with* the perceived trend and played the hot machines, or he went *against* the perceived trend and played the due machines because they had to become hot, right? Of course, there is no such thing as a predictable trend in random games and those slots are random. The hot machines can stay hot or turn cold or do everything in between. The due machines can become hot or stay cold or do everything in between too.

Despite gamblers' hunger for finding some sense in randomness and past trends, there is none. It is a fool's errand to speculate how the machines will pay out—except to understand the statistics behind how a machine functions. But even the programmers of the machines can't predict what will happen next or in the near future. These machines will range from cold to hot in an unpredictable way. That's randomness in a nutshell.

By the way, these signs explained exactly what was meant by "hot" and what was meant by "due." There was no attempt to fool players, even though the advertising did play into most slot players' fantasies of getting on a predictable winning streak or hot machine.

Player's Cards

To encourage their players to return time and again to their specific properties, casinos will issue player's cards (also known as "comp cards") to reward their players for ultimately losing their money. These rewards are in the form of cash back, free play, meals, rooms, and—for those high rollers—well, they can get everything the casino has to offer. Naturally the casino is giving back a percentage of a player's *theoretical* loss. While slot clubs generally talk in terms of points, these points are determined based on a single criteria: how much money a player puts through the machine and what percentage that machine is programmed to keep over time.

Casinos realize that most slot players will "churn" their money through the machine over and over. Players will win some money and play that money; if they win some more money, they will play that money too. The original stake of the player goes through the machine, and the wins go through the machine as well. That can total up to a lot of money. All of that money is counted as "cash in," and all comps are based on how much total cash the player puts into the machine. The house has an edge on all that money and expects that over time a player will lose a theoretical percentage of all the money a player puts through their machines. They will give players comps based on this theoretical long-term loss.

There is nothing to be lost from using a player's club card. The casino wants to reward players for their play, so why not let them? It's nice for players to get something back for the risks—and losses—they are taking playing those machines. So get a card and put it into the machine every time you play. Low rollers' play is not insubstantial either, because these slot-club points can add up no matter what denomination the machine being played. And again, these comps are based on theoretical losses over the long run, not on what a player wins or loses on a given night or in her whole history with an individual casino.

"Near Miss" Machines

These machines have been outlawed in most jurisdictions. They were programmed to put winning symbols for jackpots on the line above the decision line to make the players think that they had just gotten "this close" to winning a big chunk of change. Of course, the player didn't miss anything by "this much" because those symbols would not have been on the player's line once her symbols had been selected by the RNG. But the machine was programmed to insert them just above the player's decision line to feed his hunger to win those big payouts. The "Near Miss" machines would spur the players to play more and more as they thought, *Gee, I'm getting so close. Sooner or later I'm bound to hit. I am definitely going to get hot on this machine. Look how close I keep coming!*

It is also possible that in the normal course of slot play, winning jackpot symbols will appear on the lines you aren't playing. In a random game, such results will happen, but that is far different from a slot machine being deliberately programmed to sucker the player into playing more by *consistently* landing winning symbols just above the actual decision line.

Tournament Play

If you put in some time at a given casino, it is quite possible that you will be invited to play in its tournaments. The machines used in tournaments are not typical slot machines—they are looser than loose. There is only one real strategy in slot tournaments: hit the play button as fast as you can to get in as many decisions as possible—the slot machine carpal tunnel syndrome. The more decisions, the better, because the winner of the tournament is the individual who wins the most credits—thus fast, faster, and fastest is the best way to play in a tournament.

CHAPTER 4

The New In-Between Machines

If you think of the stereotypical slot-machine player, you might picture a lone wolf, slyly scouring the slot aisles for her perfect machine, loving the fact that she will play completely alone and anonymously and rarely have to be bothered by annoying players intruding on her time of enjoyment.

Slot-machine fun has traditionally been looked at as solitary fun. You and your slot machine, bound together forever...or until you move to another machine. Fidelity in slot-machine play is definitely not a standard player behavior, nor is shared play with another player who might be several inches away.

But today a host of new machines, often called "community machines" or "community slot machines" have been coming onto the casino floors and combine machine play with the table-game experience because several to dozens of players can play these machines at the same time in the same place. The games are not interactive in the sense of one player playing against another player, as traditional poker would be. But all players have a common focal point and often shared jackpots.

They are all playing a game that somehow binds them together. While one can make a case that the traditional progressive slot machines are also "community machines" because every player is looking to hit the same top jackpot, the game is played just like any other slot machine, and the machines can be in various areas of the casino or the casino town. There is no real sense of community or comradeship in the playing of these typical linked-progressive machines.

As of this writing I have seen community machines of craps, black-jack, Pai Gow poker, roulette, Wheel of Fortune, and Monopoly. There are many others on the drawing boards as well.

Some of these games, such as roulette, will actually have a dealer running them. However, the players make all their bets on a computer screen, just like video poker, not on the felt of an actual table. All the players will be seated at their individual machines in a giant circle around the dealer and the roulette machine. When the ball goes around and around on the screen, all the players watch the same images to see what the decision is and who has won or lost.

Players don't have to worry about buying chips, redeeming chips, or dropping their chips. Players do not have to dodge one another to get their bets down, and the game goes far faster than the average traditional table-game version. At the community roulette tables that I have seen, there has been plenty of action for the casino. So it looks as if this machine may be a keeper for the house. The players like the cleanness of the game, and the casino likes the speed, because the speedier the game, the more money the casino makes from that game.

I recently played a blackjack machine that had five seats for the players and a giant video screen that showed an animated and very friendly dealer. By the way, machine dealers never have off days or less-than-stellar personalities. She dealt the cards and gave all us players a moment to think about hitting, standing, doubling, or splitting. The game paid 3-to-2 for blackjacks, which made it as good as any single-deck game found on the casino floor. And the dealer smiled all the time too.

Of course, on this community blackjack game, no player can get a real edge because the deck is shuffled after every hand, and it is impossible to count cards. Still, the house edge was in the tenths of a percent, making it a really good game. There is a caveat here, though. This game, just as the above roulette game, is much faster than a normal traditional game played at a real table. The casino gets in many more hands, and that small edge is sharpened because of the increased speed of the game. When I played this game, all five player spots were taken. Again, this might also be a keeper for the casinos.

I have not been satisfied with the community craps games I have seen. There is just not the kind of excitement during the game as there is in the real table game. Everyone at the community craps game knows the machine is completely random, and there is no real communal sense among the players. Yes, the real game of craps is also completely random with the exception of the infinitesimal number of Golden Touch controlled shooters out there. However, there is a powerful sense that the shooters in the real game of craps have some control over what they are doing. That "sense" might be nonsense, but it adds to the heart-thumping excitement of the real table game. So I think the machine craps game is going to be a big failure.

Rumor has it that the slot manufacturers are contemplating bringing in some of the fun board games that the 1950s, 1960s, and 1970s generations have played, including Monopoly (I've seen WMS's community Monopoly), Risk, Scrabble, and Parcheesi. I'm actually hoping we can see some community machine games where players actually compete against other players. If I win, I take your credits; you win, you take my credits. (Or maybe that would cause fights? Although that might be considered an added entertainment value.)

Now, many inveterate traditional slot players look askance at these community machines, thinking of them more as table games than as slot-machine games. So they sniff with distaste as they pass them and head off into the "real" slot aisles. The reverse is also true. Many table-game players look askance at these machine games because they think of them as slots and not as real table games. They snort at them as they scurry past them to head for the tables.

Yet there is a growing nexus of people who do not identify themselves as strictly table-game players or strictly slots players. These are the players who will make or break the community slot-machine experience.

I think it would probably be fun to give some time to these games, as you might find them different from your normal routine and maybe even more exciting. You have nothing to lose other than some money, but that goes for traditional slots and traditional table games as well.

CHAPTER 5

Money Management
at Slots

I f someone gave you $1,000 to play in a casino slot machine, what strategy would be the best to increase the likelihood of coming home with a win? Would you put all of it in a $1,000-per-spin machine and take your shot with one and only one spin? Or would you divide your money up and play all of it over the course of several sessions or days?

So which do you choose?

Many players don't know this, but the math is very clear on the subject. In games where the house has the edge—and it does have the edge on almost all slots on each and every spin—you are better off putting all of your money through the machine at once. So the $1,000-per-spin machine is the best machine for your $1,000. The math of slot play makes a loss more certain as time goes on because that house edge eats away at the money being played the way the ocean eats away at the rocks on the shore—the ocean is relentless and so are house edges. You might not see the ocean's wear on those rocks but the erosion is taking place every moment a wave hits them. So as more and more players dump their thousand bucks into the machines all over the earth, the house edge is going to decimate the money played in those machines because so many decisions are being made.

But in reality the math is *emotionally* wrong because slot players are not computers or calculators or emotionless machines plugging away at the mathematically correct way to do things. If slot players were finely calculated machines, they wouldn't play the negative-expectation slot machines. You are unlikely to find a slot player anywhere on earth who would get a sustained thrill depositing all of his or her gambling money into the machines in one lump sum. That's not why they play. They play because they *like* to *play*! One bet is just not that satisfying.

Most slot players, if not all slot players, enjoy the ins and outs, the ups and downs, and the unceasing search for the hot machines as much as they enjoy the occasional win and the infrequent or rare windfall. "Doing it" at the slots is as important as the final results of one's play—slot-machine play is foreplay with an occasional big score. For slot players, the journey is as important as the fantasized destination: a nice win—or any win, for that matter.

So while the math of gambling says clearly to put all your money into the machine at once, the reality of slot play is much different. We want our money to s-t-r-e-t-c-h so that our time at the machines stretches too. Playing a little is fun; playing a lot is more fun.

To do that, we must manage our money in such a way that we don't lose too much of it too soon, even if the machines are being particularly unkind to us during our sessions. Being a good money manager at slots does take some realignment of one's ideas—especially about the denomination of the machines one plays. Slot players will often give themselves much less money than they need to last very long at the machines they are playing. For example, if you have $100 to put through the machines, you had better consider playing three nickels or one quarter at a time. Even so, a bad streak will see you with not much in reserve to launch a comeback. As we all know, slots are hungry devils, and they can go through our money the way a school of piranha can go through a fat cow.

So let me set up a scenario for you that will give you the most protection for your bankroll and the ability to last at the machines to enjoy all the ups and downs and ins and outs, which, for most slot players, add up to the fun of playing the machines.

Let us say that you want to play four hours in each of three straight days in your favorite casino. How much money do you need to bring to the casino to weather the worst of all possible scenarios—losing every single spin? If we postulate spinning the reels once every 10 seconds—a rather relaxed pace—then we will lose six spins per minute, 360 spins per hour, 1,440 spins in one day, and 4,320 spins over the course of the three days.

If you want to play for three days *guaranteed*, then give yourself enough money to do those 4,320 spins—and that would certainly be worriless slot play, as no bad streak could wipe you out. You'd never have to kick yourself in your derriere for losing all your money right away because you have enough money to give you all the action you crave over the time you plan to be playing.

At quarter machines, playing one quarter at a time, you will need $1,080 for your three days. Double that at a 50¢ machine, while at a dollar machine you'll need $4,320, and at a $5 machine you'll need a whopping $21,600. I realize this is an "end-of-the-world" type of bank-roll sizing, but it does do one very glorious thing—it guarantees that you can play for the amount of time you wish to play without ever having to worry about going completely broke and ending your casino sojourn prematurely. And the chances of losing every single one of those 4,320 spins would be unheard of.

If you are looking to make your money last, then the machines you select should also figure into the equation. On any denomination machine, avoid the linked progressives, as the house edges on them are usually in the double digits. Stick to stand-alone machines that distribute the jack-pots equally. Thus, the top jackpot line might pay 200 coins for one coin, 400 coins for two coins, and 600 coins for three coins. You get no extra benefit by putting your money in three times faster on such machines, so it makes sense to play just that one coin. Doing this stretches your time, but it does not stretch your risk.

I realize that many slot players don't have my Armageddonish view of money management and are willing to risk a better chance of going broke than I am. If so, then cut my advice in half. Have $540 to play one coin in a 25¢ machine, for example.

Let me reiterate something that many slot players tend to forget as they pump up the steam engine of their slot play: playing fast is bad, while playing slow is good. The tendency for most slot players I have seen is to start off slowly, leisurely spinning those reels, but as their time at the machines increases, so does their speed of play. That's a prescription for bankroll disaster. Playing slots with increasing speed is similar to a drinker. The first drink is sipped slowly, the second somewhat faster, and by the tenth drink, our connoisseur is pouring the fiery liquid down his throat until he pukes on everyone within eight feet and then passes out in a giant heap.

Having enough money to play the amount of time you wish to play is important, but it is equally important to keep the totality of spins within some reasonable range.

Now what if you are the kind of player who becomes ferociously fast as time wears on or the liquor heats you up until you catch fire? You just can't help yourself, in other words. Playing slots is like running downhill; it's fast, faster, and fastest. If you are a speedster, then you have to stand up every few spins and stretch your body. You have to find ways to take time away from spinning those reels. Sitting in front of the machine just makes you want to spin those reels like dervishes. But standing up every five or 10 spins and stretching or looking around will give you a needed way to reduce the number of decisions that you are facing due to your speeding.

That might sound stupid, but as Forrest Gump's mother used to say, "Stupid is as stupid does." Playing fast is doing the wrong thing, and taking steps to reduce your speed—even if that means stepping away from the machine for a few seconds every so often—is a smart move.

So let me lay out my super plan for semiperfect slot play—although my plan obviously can't guarantee you a win if you are playing a negative-expectation slot machine.

1. Do not play any progressive slot machines. While the average of the quarter machines might be a 90 percent return, factored into that average are all those progressives where the return is much worse. If you stick to playing nonprogressives, you will most likely increase the return percentage for yourself.

2. Only play one coin in the machine per decision. While many slot players think that playing full coin is the way to go, the fact is that you are playing three credits to increase the payback by a

fractional percentage, as most slot machines only reward you if you hit the big jackpot. That fractional increase in return doesn't make up for the fact that you are putting in three times more money with each spin. Better still, select an equal-distribution machine that does not reward you for extra coins played.

3. Reduce how many spins you play. Instead of playing 12 spins per minute, play six to eight spins per minute. This reduces your expected losses dramatically.

4. Bring enough money to last the entire time you wish to play. Or divide your money up into session stakes with the imperative, "I will not lose more than this amount for this session."

5. Avoid all those small-change games that make you want to play dozens of coins. Eschew the new penny and nickel machines. They are deadly for your bankroll.

One last thing: always use your player's club card in the slot machines, because doing so is added value. You want to get all the cash back, comps, and gifts the casino is willing to give you for playing their machines. Use my Armageddon money-management formula, and your slot fun will stretch nicely over time. Either that, or put all your money in at once... and pray!

CHAPTER 6

Quit While You're Ahead and Other Impossibilities

"I should have quit while I was ahead." You have heard this line time and again from depressed, whimpering slots players. Or you've heard really disgruntled slots players complaining, "I gave back all the money I won in the beginning! Why didn't I quit when I was ahead?"

You've read what many gambling writers have written: "Always quit when you are ahead." And you might even have nodded your head in agreement when you read that or heard sad slot players saying that.

"Yes, of course, you should always quit when you are ahead," you might have said to yourself as you ventured into the casino to play the machines. But did that dictum have any real influence over how you actually played? I think not—even if, at this moment, you might have thought so. And I think I can convincingly prove my case.

"Quit while you are ahead" is almost as famous a saying as, "I did not have sex with that woman" and "I am not a crook" or "There will be peace in our time." It is also just as false as these other statements.

At first these words make sense; I'll admit that too. Why not quit while you are ahead? But if you look at the actual meaning behind those words, you will see that for the overwhelming majority of slot players it is impossible to quit while they are ahead for a variety of reasons, not the least of which being the fact that they were never ahead during any portion of their play.

Let's take a look at the other problems of actually quitting while you are ahead. Let's speculate that the average "hit" frequency for a slot machine in this example is somewhere between 9 and 21 percent—so let's average that out and make the "hit" frequency 15 percent. We will ignore the fact that sometimes a hit is not a win (you play three coins and get two back—while that is a "hit," it is not a win) and pretend that 15 percent of all spins are actually wins.

Now using the Einsteinium "thought experiment" model let us postulate that all the players in the casino start playing at the exact same time. When they are finished with that first decision, an average of 15 percent of them are winners. And here is the first rub. Should they immediately stop playing, take their win, and go home—even if home is hundreds or thousands of miles away? Quitting while you are ahead means heading the hell out of Lady Luck's domain with your win.

You see the dilemma. They have saved up their money for a wonderful time in their favorite casino venue, but fate intervened, darn it. They won their first spin, and now they must head home because they are ahead.

"George, pack up the bags, we're heading back to Duluth!"

"But Martha, I just unpacked!"

And what about the other 85 percent of the slot players who are now behind after their first spin? On the next spin of the reels, some of them might win enough to be ahead, but most of them will still be behind. The ones who are ahead now must leave if they wish to follow the dictum of quitting while they are ahead. And the others now must...what? Play until they get ahead—which is unlikely for almost all of them—or until they lose every penny they have brought with them. "Sal, honey, please mortgage the house because I will only quit when I am ahead, and I'm not ahead yet!"

That is not a pretty picture. It is also not a picture based at all on the reality of casino slot play. Naturally everyone reading this book is no idiot when it comes to slot play and slot players. You know slot players as well as I do. No slot player I know is going to quit while ahead after the first spin or the second spin or the third spin—unless one of those spins wins Megabucks and the player has to wait for all the happy casino executives to certify the win, have their pictures snapped with the overwhelmed winner, and tell the government that it is sharing in the jackpot. In fact, most slot players wish to spend *time* at the machines. That is their aim—playing first, winning second.

Yes, all slot players would like to win tonight, that's true, but winning tonight is actually not as important to them as playing tonight; thus, playing tonight trumps winning tonight in all slot players' minds. So the dictum "Quit while you are ahead" sounds good, but it has nothing to do with the reality of playing slot machines. Only a complete lunatic would fly to Las Vegas, drive to Atlantic City, or head down the road to his or her local gambling palace, win on the very first spin, and turn around and go back home. It would be interesting to know if any of my readers have met such a lunatic. I haven't.

So what is the unvarnished truth of slot players and winning? Varied, to say the least. The fact is that the overwhelming majority of slot players plan their play sessions on a sort of continuum of experience mixed with economic reality. Some players dictate that they will play for several hours and, win or lose, quit after that time; some dictate to themselves that they will play until they lose all their money or are so tired that, win or lose, they will drag themselves to bed or be carried to bed by the security guards or be ambulanced to the local emergency room suffering from what is known as "the Vegas flu."

Some slot players will play a certain number of spins; some will say to themselves, "If I win $300, I am quitting until my next session, but if I lose $200, I will quit until my next session." Some players give themselves X amount to play with each day, and that is all they will play—whether in one long session, several medium sessions, or many short sessions. If they lose that X, then they are finished for that day, even if that X gave them dissatisfaction in terms of time. If they win after their planned sessions or because they are exhausted or because they have lost that X, then that is that for that day.

Okay, now is there a proper way to play the slot machines? Probably not. Proper slot play, with the exception being those advantage machines in Chapter 24, is another impossibility in the real world. We all have our own ideas of what is fun. I am not fond of the idea of playing until I collapse and then having to be dragged to bed. I like to be wide awake when I play in the casinos. Not all players are interested in being fully conscious when at the machines, and they have the right to be semiconscious or almost unconscious, too. To each his or her own unique playing style—even if that style is totally idiotic.

It is another impossibility to force people to play as you want them to play. Trust me, I know this for a fact, since I have been writing about slot machines for more than two decades. Players play the way they want to play—whether it agrees with the way I want them to play or not. Of course, I am right....

I have many friends who are gambling writers, and they are fun, intelligent, and humble people—but after all, they are—when all is said and done—merely writing about games that people play. They aren't discovering cures for cancer or ways to get into the far reaches of outer space. Gambling is fun, and writing about gambling is also fun. That's the skinny.

I have one acquaintance who just started his career as a slot writer for a small slot publication. He is a bright young man with a master's degree in mathematics, and he is being driven insane by the reactions to his public speeches and by letters and emails from his readers.

"I give out the best information about the slot machines in my articles and my talks," he told me one day. "I tell the slot players which machines are the best to play and which machines are the worst to play based on their overall payback percentages. I explain in very simple terms the math of the machines and how all paybacks will affect your long-run prospects. I explain hit frequency and the RNG. I go step-by-step through everything. And you know what? They argue with me when I give talks!"

He continued, "Some will tell me that they heard from someone who knows these things that on each machine is a little code of numbers, and when those numbers get higher the machine is about to pay off. When I ask who this person in the know is, they tell me that he is a longtime slot player who knows his stuff. I explain that this is a false notion, and they look at me as if I am crazy. I used to work for a slot company, for crying out loud!"

Poor kid, he is learning the hard way that not all slot players are interested in his scientific information on the machines. Many slot players—although few who read this particular book, I might add—have idiosyncratic views of how the machines work and why and when these machines will pay off.

The ranges of beliefs concerning slot machines can often go from the plain silly to the astoundingly dumb. Some players believe that if a slot machine has just hit a big jackpot, it is likely to hit again very soon because the machine is now hot. Some believe the opposite, that a machine that has just hit will go cold because of that specific hit. We know that machines aren't hot or cold; they are just pumping out their programming. If a big Megabucks jackpot is a 1 in 50 million event, it is a 1 in 50 million event every time the reels are spun. It might be possible that two of these jackpots will hit in a row or a short period of time, but no matter—it is always a 50 million-to-1 shot.

Certainly machines sometimes pay out a lot in a small period of time, and certainly they sometimes seem like skinflints paying small amounts over long periods of time—but randomness always has odd patterns, and what you see in this or that string of decisions is randomness at work.

Some players think the actual feel of a machine can help them determine whether the machine will hit or not. Some players think that if the machine is hot to the touch, it will get hot—while other players, equally fervent in their beliefs, think that machine will get cold. Some players think that if the machine is cool to the touch, it will get cold—others believe it will get hot. If the machine is dented, it is a cold machine because someone punched it—or it is a hot machine because someone belted it with joy after a big win.

My acquaintance finally asked me, "Why don't people listen to me?"

I told him to think back to his school days. How many students actively listened to everything a teacher said? Few or none—otherwise everyone would have a 99 or 100 average. How many students used study hall to study and not daydream? Few or none.

I am reminded of a bible story. Moses has just freed the slaves from Egypt, after God did 10 miracles, finally drowning the Pharaoh's *entire army* in the Red Sea, the waters of which God has just parted for His people to walk across. Moses taught his people a valuable lesson about the power of God, didn't he?

Then Moses tells them to wait for him because he is going up the mountain and not to violate any of God's commands. He goes up the mountain, and what do many of his students do? Everything Moses told them *not* to do.

I explained this to my young acquaintance. I said, "If Moses couldn't teach everyone, and he had God's help, don't feel bad because you can't teach everyone either." It's a good lesson to learn.

Since I rarely play any machines that have a house edge over me, I don't worry about my money. I play basically only the advantage-play machines when they are in a positive mode. I've never said otherwise. But slot players have minds and desires of their own. Some use their play as an escape from the real world, some look at their play as an intensification of the real world, and some look at slot play as the real world and that monster jackpot as the way to make their lives livable. Again, to each his or her own, even though, I repeat, I am right.

And you know what? I hope all slot players get what they want—plenty of quality time at the machines and maybe, just maybe, the chance to quit while they are ahead as well.

CHAPTER 7

The 401G: Save Up Your Pennies

My neighbor Jane loves to take the bus down to Atlantic City every Tuesday. She has a lot of great anticipatory fun from Thursdays through Mondays ("If I win big I am going to buy myself a..."), but on Wednesdays, the day after her weekly trip, she is usually complaining that she could have used the money she lost for something else. "Do you know I could have gone to see a Broadway play and brought my sister, too, with that money I lost?"

Jane could have seen every show on Broadway with the money she spent on the slot machines in Atlantic City, by her account.

I usually cite the instantaneous transference of gambling money into real money once the gambling money has been lost as a very bad sign for the gambler. It means you are gambling with money you shouldn't be gambling with. As soon as you say or think, "I could have done thus and such with that money instead of gambling it away," that means trouble. Using real money for gambling money is a poor choice.

Gambling money should have no impact on your life. If you go to the casinos every Tuesday and lose each and every Tuesday, never even winning one time (which probably won't happen in your lifetime), the money lost shouldn't even enter your consciousness. Such money is just gambling money. It isn't real.

However, if the money you lost suddenly causes you to think, *Gee, I could have paid for my brain surgery with that!* then you had better

39

sit down and do some serious thinking about your pastime. Only a fool gambles money that should have been used for something else.

It took me several years to realize that I needed to create a separate account for my gambling money. This was in the mid-1980s. And by a separate account, I mean a totally separate *bank account*. I opened a money-market checking account that got me decent interest, and I put my initial gambling stake in it. That stake was a mere $5,000—but it started me going. In those days, I was the lowest of low rollers.

By having that 401G account (my name for a gambling account, as the *G* stands for *Gambling*), my losses didn't start me panicking that I was using my "heart surgery" money on something so frivolous as a gambling game.

If you have plenty of money, just take a percent of it and place it into your new 401G account. From this point on, you only gamble against that account. As the money declines, as it will unless you only play advantage machines, then you put some more in. Again, this will be money you don't need for your brain surgery.

Many players don't have money to immediately set aside for their 401G. That's fine. If you work a regular job, you should begin to take a small percentage of your weekly salary and put it in the account—every week without fail. It might be $100 a week, or more, or less. When that account gets to $2,000, then you can become a quarter player, playing one quarter per spin on nonprogressive machines, preferably equal-distribution machines. That gives you 8,000 spins of the reels on your next trip to the casino if you wish to use all your money through the machine one time. You can divide how you play your money however you wish. It could be one long session, a few shorter ones, or many tiny ones—your choice.

After those 8,000 spins—win, lose, or draw—you are done for that visit. You take whatever money is left and put it all back into the 401G.

Or you could take $2,000 and play for two hours, however many spins that is, and—win or lose—call it a day. The object here is to grow the gambling account to such an extent that after a while you can play longer and longer because the losses just won't cut into the account all that much—assuming you keep yourself under control, that is.

As your account grows, which it will because you are making steady contributions to it, then you can increase your time at the machines. But stick to playing quarters until you get the 401G up to $20,000. Then you can go to a single 50¢ machine. At $30,000, you can play a single dollar. At $60,000 you can start on a $5-per-spin machine.

You'll note that your increase in machine denomination does not follow a straight multiple because the higher the denomination the greater the return. A $5 machine will usually return about 94–96 percent of the money played in it, whereas quarter machines will return about 90 percent. That extra return means you don't need as much money to play these machines—you just need enough so several bad sessions won't start you thinking about doing something else with the money.

If you strictly play advantage machines, you will probably win money over time, and these wins should be socked back into your account. Although many of the advantage-play machines are in the 25¢–$1 range, the profits can be quite hefty if these are the only machines you play.

So the bottom line is to keep your surgery money in one account and your gambling dollars in another account—and never should those accounts meet. It's healthier that way.

CHAPTER 8
Moola or Markers?

Money may be the root of all evil, but it is also the root of all casino gambling as well. The saying is simply, "No pay, no play."

But how do you pay? In the good old days, you just put your coins in and spun the reels, then put in more coins and spun the reels. In the not-quite-so-old days, you could pile up credits and play with those—you didn't have to keep feeding the machines with coins, at least not as long as you had some credits remaining.

Today you have the benefits of credits, and you also don't have to deal with those dirty coins that discolor your fingers, because so many machines are now the newfangled coinless machines that sometimes (poorly) attempt to mimic the sound effects of the old machines.

The big question for many slot players today no longer revolves around which machines they will play but rather how to put the money in them. More specifically, does one bring cash to the casinos to feed the metallic beasts, or does one establish credit with the casinos so he or she can take out markers?

A cash player usually has a set limit of money to play with, and once that is gone, the player is usually gone too. The chance to go on tilt and to throw more money after losing money is not too great a danger unless the player looks to those ATM or credit-card machines.

The second way to handle playing money is to establish credit with the casino. Many slot players don't realize the casinos will give them credit to play the machines. This means you don't have to carry wads of cash with you.

Casinos look favorably on credit players because they figure, usually correctly, that whatever the player has as his or her total credit line is what the player is willing to lose. With cash players, the casinos are not always sure of just how deep into their pockets these people will go.

Establishing casino credit is quite easy. While different jurisdictions have slightly different forms and questions—with Atlantic City probably being the most rigorous of the venues and Vegas being the most lenient—the bottom line for the casinos is simple: do you have enough money in the bank account you are using to pay whatever markers you take out? A marker is a check that you sign that can be deposited in your account. If you have the money, you usually get the credit—although many casinos will give you slightly less credit than you asked for. If you really can afford to lose $10,000, you should probably ask for $15,000 since there is a good chance you will only be given $10,000.

Credit players are courted by the casinos because they are players who seem to be more committed to play than most cash players. After all, if you are asking for credit, the assumption on the part of the casino credit manager is that you are going to be, or currently are, a steady player in their casino.

With the multistate and multicasino empires that have been established by certain megacompanies, getting credit at one of the properties makes it easier to get credit at another of the properties. This can help you in planning your casino vacations. You'll tend to go to the casinos where you have such credit.

The biggest danger for credit players has to do with going too deeply into their bankroll to play the machines. If you have a $5,000 credit line, but you really shouldn't play more than $1,000 on any given trip, the urge might be there to "just dip in a little more" to make a comeback. Credit players have to train themselves to handle credit just the way they handle cash: cautiously.

Once you have your credit, how do you get the money to actually play the machines? Just walk up to the cage and tell the teller you want a marker to play the machines! The teller will do the paperwork, you'll sign your marker, and the teller will then give you the money you asked for. That's it. You then take the money to the machines and play to your heart's content or discontent.

Once you are finished playing, if you have won, you should pay back your marker immediately. Casinos don't like winning players to "walk with the money." If you have lost all of the marker, then you will have two to six weeks to pay, depending on how big a credit line you have. If you have a certain amount of the marker left but not all of it, you should immediately pay what you can and then pay the rest in the allotted time.

Only you can decide if you wish to be a credit player or a cash player. I prefer to play with a credit line because I don't like to walk around with too much cash on me. I don't have the ubiquitous problem of "taking just a little more to make a comeback" since I did that once at the beginning of my playing career and got severely burned. I learn my lessons fast.

Credit play can be a great alternative for many slot players. It certainly is something you should consider if you can handle it.

CHAPTER 9
Loose Machines

You are well aware of the fact that the higher the denomination of the machine, the better chance those machines are looser than the denominations below them. This fact is called the Higher Denomination Machines are Looser Law.

You also know that the big progressive machines such as Megabucks, Wheel of Fortune, and Quartermania (and so on) are much tighter than nonprogressive stand-alone machines. The law behind this fact is called the Big Jackpot Machines Ain't Looser Law.

Just about every gambling writer on earth explains these facts in many different ways, over and over, in order to make your slot play return more of your money to you or lose you less of your money, which is the more accurate statement. After all, the money is better in your pocket or purse than in those large casino vaults that are under the ground of every casino.

But no one knows about other types of loose machines. Only I know which stand-alone machines are looser than other stand-alone machines.

Now *you* will know this too, because I am a generous guy, and I want to see you all have a better chance to take home the casino's money—or, at the very least, take home some of the money you brought to the casino to play the slot machines. To do that, I have to reveal this secret to you right now; otherwise you would have to wait until my next book.

But before I reveal this secret to you, let me explain something about the difference between you and the casinos. They are richer than you.

Yes, even if you are rich compared to other human beings, you are not as rich as the casinos. If you look at their table games closely, you will note that the floor person is always trying to get those games to run faster in order to get more decisions in. The more decisions that a game has, the better it is for the casino because the house edge grinds away that way. It's the math of the game, and the math works out in reality when more and more decisions take place.

Okay, in simple words, fast games with a lot of decisions are good for the casino. Less-fast games with fewer decisions are less good for the casinos. You might well notice—if you are really sharp—that good and less good are *both* still good for the casino. That's the sorry truth of negative-expectation casino games. They are all good for the casino—it's just that some are *more good* than others.

Using this knowledge of fast is good, we turn our attention to the slot machines, which is the game of your choice. Everything is reversed in the world of slots. That's the trick! If a slot machine is very fast coming up with decisions, the casino doesn't have to take as much money from each and every spin because you are going to have many, many more spins for the house edge to eat away at you.

So faster slot machines are looser.

However, if the slot machine is slow with decisions because there are all sorts of display creations and cute figures doing cute things, the house has to increase their edge on these machines so that the casinos still make the kind of money they desire from them—or rather from you, actually, since you are the one pumping your money into them.

So slower slot machines are tighter.

Okay, those are general principles, but how do you tell which are fast machines and which are slow machines? This isn't easy; you have to *play* them! ("Oh, the agony!") Let's say that when a certain machine hits certain pay lines, tiny little cute creatures come dancing and singing and mating on the screen, taking up a lot of time. Then you have another machine that doesn't have tiny little cute creatures or even big ugly creatures or any other entertainment segment—the reels spin, you learn your fate, and you spin them again.

The machine that has an entertainment component is probably going to be tighter than the machine without the entertainment component. So don't play those machines; just play the nonentertainment ones.

But why play the other machine, which is faster and therefore still loses you more money in the long run because of its speed? I am glad you asked that question.

Unlike table games, where the dealer has something to say about the speed of the game, you can still play those faster machines slower! Do you have that? *Play the fast machines slow!* Reduce the number of decisions on them, and now you are playing a loose machine slowly and getting more pleasure out of it. At least I am guessing you'll get more pleasure out of it—unless you are insane and enjoy losing faster on those faster machines when you should be playing slowly.

Now I do not have absolute proof that what I am saying about playing fast machines slowly is the way to go or that I am correct in my assumptions. In fact, I have no current proof that what I am saying is correct... except that about 20 years ago my wife, the beautiful AP, and I did a little experiment in Vegas. We played side-by-side machines—of different types—putting in the exact same amount of money the exact same way. We'd play the machines for an hour and then see what kind of comps we had racked up. We *never* had the same amount in comps! I assumed that the machines that were looser were paying back less in comps and the machines that were tighter were paying back more in comps. Something had to explain why one machine would give back more in comps and the other machine would give back less in comps with the exact same amount of money played in each of them for the exact same amount of time.

Using that little experiment as a guide, I am thinking that my current theory is correct also. If it is, you will save money by playing fast machines slowly. And if I'm wrong—well, you aren't going to lose any more money than you would have lost had you played the way you always do.

Go to it, boys and girls!

CHAPTER 10

Many Small Wins versus a Few Big Wins

I've had the good fortune to do consulting work for some of the biggest slot manufacturers in the country, and often this work will come down to the following question: "Should we program our machines so slot players get many small wins but therefore extremely few big wins, or do we program our machines so slot players get very few small wins but more big wins?"

This question is almost unanswerable in the aggregate, because what slot player #1 wants is not necessarily what slot player #2 wants. Obviously when you walk around the casino floor you will note machines with high hit frequencies and machines with low hit frequencies. Usually machines with low hit frequencies are the ones that give out more big wins but fewer small wins, while machines with large hit frequencies tend to give out many more small wins but much fewer big wins.

Obviously my answer to the above profound slot question—it being intellectually well considered after decades of experience in the slot business and blazing insight into the minds of slot players—is, I have no idea! Although the majority of players—a slight majority, I must add—prefer large jackpots, it is a close contest. So I tell such manufacturers to do both! Have some machines that reward on a consistent basis with a lot of small wins, and have some machines that will lose spin after spin after spin and then explode with a big winner.

As I view it, there are fundamentally two types of savvy slot players—those who are looking for consistency in their machines and those who are looking to jump up and down and scream their lungs out when they get those nice payouts. The former is looking to have much more back-and-forth with the machine, and the latter is looking to experience the adrenaline rush of a big win. I guess you could also list a third type of slot player: the player who doesn't have any idea of what he or she actually wants and wanders around playing whatever slot happens to hit his or her fancy. These players are legion too.

Interestingly enough, some new mega-multiline machines can give the slot player a taste of both the good hit frequency but small wins (you get a hit but no win, just some credits back) and also the thrill of occasional big wins when you get a hit and the credit meter goes nuts.

There is a major difference between slot players and table-game players in the area of wins and losses. Table-game players always expect close contests between themselves and the casinos. Blackjack players win about 44 percent of their hands and lose about 48 percent, with 8 percent being pushes. Outside bettors at roulette expect an almost 50–50 winning percentage against the house (it's actually 20 losses to 18 wins), and smart craps players expect an almost 50–50 split on the best bets (actually 251 losses to 244 wins). While there are some "long shots" at table games, these are nowhere near the type of "long shots" you find on slot machines.

Because traditional slot players (i.e., those who play three-reel machines) have been trained over the years to accept many losing decisions in a row, even on machines with high hit frequencies, they are willing to be patient, which means they can tolerate long losing streaks without panicking or throwing their hands up in disgust and running out of the casino howling in agony. Indeed, the players who want to hit it big have monumental patience and will go 30 or 40 spins without a hit because they are sure the big one is just around the corner. That corner is often very far away, too—like in another city.

Most traditional slot machines have hit frequencies of between 9 and 25 percent. Now think of losing 91 percent of your spins, because that is what 9 percent means. That is some losing quotient. Even an 80 percent loss quotient would hit savvy table-game players right between the eyes—they would think they are being cheated. Imagine a blackjack player consistently losing 80 percent of his or her hands, which would be staggering. At 91 percent, the blackjack player would probably run from the table screaming that the game was fixed.

Not so with well-trained slot players. They have the patience of Job. And they need it. However, even on the tightest slot machines, those big wins keep them playing. That is the secret of these machines' success.

The slot player who prefers the "give-and-take" finds the high-hit-frequency machines to his or her liking. This player has a better chance of coming home with a win tonight, although that win is probably somewhat pedestrian.

The gap between the two types of savvy slot players is quite large, indeed. So what kind of slot player are you?

CHAPTER 11
Winning the Big One

Dream a Little Dream with Me!

I confess! When the New York State Lottery gets to $60 million, I will buy tickets. When the Mega Millions lottery gets to $200 million, I will buy tickets. Being a stolid, solid gambler I try to put myself in a good position to overcome the house edge; yes, even on lottery tickets there are better and worse times to make bets.

So the lottery amounts above make the game a good bet, because they are greater than the odds of hitting them. The New York State Lottery is about 35 million–to-1, and Mega Millions is about 150 million–to-1.

So why even bother spending money on the lotteries as I do on those rare occasions when they hit the necessary payback levels? Isn't it just a waste to play such mega-longshot bets, even if the expectation overall is positive at least until that *other* person or people hit it? I don't kid myself into thinking I will be that person. I have never been that person, even on little lotteries I buy for charity.

On those times I play the lottery, I play it in order to dream monstrously large dreams. There aren't any people I know who don't want to have more money than they do now. Certainly a nice $60–$200 million win would put me in a category of wealth I can only dream about. So dream I do. I picture how I would spend the money, who I would help, what luxuries I would buy.

Here are some examples: I'd want a nice big ranch house on at least 125 acres. I'd want outdoor and indoor Olympic-sized swimming pools.

I'd make sure my sons never had to worry about money ever again. I'd give a sizeable chunk to certain charities for illnesses that have affected my family members—Alzheimer's, ulcerative colitis, strokes, and heart disease. There's a local nursing home run by the Little Sisters of the Poor that I would donate enough to in order to keep it going. These wonderful nuns' vocation is to take care of the indigent elderly poor.

Dreaming like this is fun, at least occasionally. It's childish, certainly, since the chances of winning are almost nil. But a little dreaming can't hurt.

And so it goes with those giant progressive slot machines you find in almost every casino in the country. Despite gambling writers such as me telling people these are very bad bets (and they are) players like to play these machines, because these are the dream machines. Walk around the casinos on a busy weekend night and most of the mega-dream machines are being played by dreamy-eyed players.

You don't have to be a mind reader to know what these players are thinking and feeling. Depending on the size of the jackpot, these dreams can go something like this:

- I'm going to tell my boss where to shove it!
- I can get a new luxury car.
- I can get a boat!
- I can send my grandchildren to college.
- I can go away to the weight-reduction clinic.
- I'm going to eat gourmet food until I explode.
- I'm going to tour Europe.
- I'm going to tour the world.
- I'm going to dump that lummox of a husband.
- My dear wife—there's the door.
- I will move to California.
- I will move away from California.
- I'll get a condo in Manhattan way up high so I can watch that skyline.
- I'm getting the hell out of New York!
- I'm going to gamble more and be treated like a king or queen by the casinos.

- I need a maid and a cook now.
- Top-shelf booze for me from now on.
- I like racehorses.
- I can't wait to see my picture in the newspapers holding that humongous check!

Yes, there are many more dreams out there in casinoland and rolling around in the heads of dreaming slot players. That may be one of the reasons the slot machines are ubiquitous.

Certainly it's hard to dream so big in a table game. After all, if you are a $10 blackjack player, the chances of hitting a big enough winning night to buy a yacht could be lower than my chances of winning one of the above lotteries.

You can win a lot of money in blackjack if you bet big and get lucky. But you have to win a lot of hands and your luck has to be extensive and prolonged to make fabulous fortunes at the game. A $1,000-a-hand blackjack player has to win for a very long time to win a million dollars. Now, if you bet $10, the most you can win on one hand is maybe $40 as you split your cards and double on the splits. In some casinos you might win $60 because you might be able to split and double three times. But you aren't going to bet $10 and win, say, $1 million dollars or $100,000 or $1,000 or $100 on that one hand. Blackjack doesn't work that way.

The most you can win on a single roulette bet of $10 is $350. The most you can win on a single craps bet of $10 is $300. These are big wins, certainly, jackpots of a kind, but they are not life altering. You might go, "Yeah!" as you hit a 35-to-1 roulette bet of $10, and you might go, "All right!" as you hit a 30-to-1 craps bet of $10. But the casino medical team isn't going to have to help you calm down after such wins, the way they might have to help someone calm down who just won a Megabucks jackpot of $20 million.

In slots, for a small investment, there is a chance for outrageous fortune. Yes, a $3 investment in a multicasino progressive could win you millions of dollars and change your life completely. The fact that such a score has odds of somewhere around 50 million–to-1 doesn't mean it can't happen—it's just very unlikely to happen, and I mean very, very, very, very, very unlikely.

But the outside—and I mean *way outside*—chance of winning a hell of a lot of money with a *seemingly* small investment fuels many slot players to play progressive machines. It is this same desire for unequaled, unearned wealth that flames the lottery bonfires across the country. In my small village, there are dozens of lottery players who play every day hoping for a big kiss from Lady Luck.

Naturally, the chance that it will be your small investment that wins dreamed-of luxuries is the trap to catch the mouse—you being that mouse. Most slot players never hit big life-altering jackpots. Some never even hit medium jackpots that make for good dinner conversation and then are quickly forgotten as the subsequent losses start to mount up.

Winning a fortune on slot play on big progressives is the stuff of golden dreams, that is true, but it isn't something that you are guaranteed no matter how much, how long, and how seriously you play. It's a lightning strike. In fact, it's much easier to get hit with lightning than to win a giant progressive slot machine. The odds of getting a royal flush in Texas Hold'em poker are 649,738-to-1. The odds of being struck by lightning in a single year are 700,000-to-1. The odds of dying in a plane crash are 11 million–to-1. The average state lottery player faces odds of 35–50 million–to-1. The Megabucks slot-machine jackpot comes in at about 50 million–to-1. The Mega Millions lottery has about 150 million–to-1 odds. And the odds of winning the Powerball jackpot are 195,249,053-to-1.

Still, those gleaming 50 million–to-1 machines hold so much promise that it is very hard for many slot players to resist them. We all want a shot at the big money.

So, in the interests of helping you fuel your "My life has changed!" dream, here is how to play the progressives if you feel you must play them. Take 10 percent of your slot-playing bankroll and dedicate this amount to the progressive machines. Play that 10 percent slowly, dreaming of what you will do with your riches once you win the big one. You can even practice saying to your boss, "Take this job and shove it!" Or you can say any one of the numerous things you might say should you win the big one.

If you play with friends or relatives (or relatives who are friends), then pool the money and double the number of spins you give your team. Let the playing of the machine be an event. In this way, you do get to dream the outlandish dream, but you don't lose too much money pursuing that dream. Oh, by the way, if you pool your money, whichever individual claims the win must pay the taxes, so you better straighten out how you are going to handle that possible nightmare.

The progressives are charming and alluring but potentially very dangerous because the house edge on these machines can be as high as 15 to 17 percent. That is an awfully large edge to overcome fueling a dream that has very little chance of becoming a reality. But if you use the 10 percent advice, you can kind of have your cake and eat it too. You can anticipate your visit to the casino and think of it as the visit that might change your life. Enjoy the anticipation.

The reason lotteries and progressive slot machines exist is for people to dream about such life-changing hits. It's fun to dream of these hits to a point, but it isn't fun to lose too much money by taking these dreams too seriously. That's nightmare territory.

Once in the casino, make that 10 percent the last money you play for your visit so that the dream can be tingling at the base of your brain for your entire visit. When you are finished playing the better-paying machines (preferably the advantage machines), whether you've won that visit or lost that visit, then go to the progressive and give it a shot.

Remember that in order to win the big jackpot you must play full coin. While I advocate playing a single coin on most slot machines, the progressives are different. The only reason to play the progressives is to hit the big one, and the only way to hit the big one is to play full coin.

The giant progressive slots have the same allure that the Sirens had for Odysseus. They promise more than they can fulfill except for the rare times when they actually give you what you want—the big score. Play them carefully so they don't blind you and wreck the ship of your bankroll.

What Not to Do When You Win

Here are some things you shouldn't do if you win the big one. I base these on actual incidents from my vast mental storehouse of actual incidents.

- Don't immediately call up your in-laws and exclaim that you are richer than thick, creamy chocolate devil's food lava cake and none of them will get a dime when you die because now you can tell them the truth—you hate them!
- Don't go around your small town shouting that you can buy and sell everyone you see.
- Don't go to the local topless joints and make a pest of yourself with the ladies. Even super-rich people can be arrested.
- Don't carry around a lot of cash that you flash so everyone respects you. If you were considered an idiot before you won those millions, you'll still be considered an idiot after you win those millions. If you flash that money, you'll be considered an even bigger idiot than you were before.
- Don't get a personalized license plate that says *I Am Rich!* or *I Can Buy and Sell You!*
- Don't invest huge chunks of your money with someone who just called you out of the blue claiming he can make you even richer.
- Don't cheat on your wife or husband because the divorce settlement will cost you at least half of the win.
- Do not allow yourself to have your picture taken holding the oversized check the casinos give you. That is an invitation for everyone on earth—and all your relatives—to find a reason to need some of your money. For some crazy reason, relatives always feel they are entitled to your good fortune.

Okay, you should call a financial planner and detail exactly how your jackpot is being paid to you and ask him or her how best to handle the money. Take your time making your plans. You might have become rich overnight, but you can become poor fairly fast too. If a financial planner comes to you first, tell him or her you already have someone you trust. (Maybe a good idea is to immediately change your phone number to an unlisted one or one listed under a fake name.) Be leery of those who call you trying to help you. You have to be aware that people will come out of the woodwork, the floorboards, and the walls wanting to help you spend your money—preferably on them.

Sadly—and truthfully—most of you reading this will never have to worry about hitting the big one, because it isn't in the cards or reels for you to do so. Lady Luck won't be your lady tonight or any night. That's a fact.

Yes, you can still dream, however, and pretend that a giant check for a giant amount is just around the bend of the next spin.

Paying the Attendant

So you win a fairly large sum of money, and soon a slot attendant arrives to either pay you or congratulate you or both. She counts out the money and gives it to you, incessantly praising your great luck or great skill or both. Then she sticks out her hand, metaphorically speaking, expecting to get a tip—like a doorman at a ritzy hotel.

Of course, the hand isn't really stretched out toward your money, but part of the payment she gives you is in small enough bills to give her a healthy tip. She's sending you a not-so-subtle signal: "Tip me. Tip me. Tip me!" Plus she just keeps standing there, smiling, waiting for you to fork over some money. Time passes. Even the biggest ploppy on earth soon realizes that the only way to get rid of this annoying well-wisher is to give her some cash.

Most slot players will do just that.

And/or, someone working the slot areas comes up to you as you wander around looking for that special machine and says, "Looking for a hot machine? That one over there," she points, "is gonna get really hot really soon. Mark my words."

Now this attendant doesn't know if the machine is going to get hot or if it is going to get cold or if it is going to get the flu or explode into a thousand pieces, killing every slot player within 50 feet. She is simply positioning herself to get a tip from you should you win a nice prize. She's probably told everyone she can that this or that machine is going to get hot. Heck, one of those machines may very well do just that. Her *playing you* is advantage gambling at its best. She risks no money but has a chance of winning some dough—*your* dough. No risk but plenty of potential gain.

And should you hit, she will be right over to say congratulations! "See, I told you that machine would get hot and make you a lot of money. I know what to look for." She sure knows what to look for—loopy players who actually believe she had something to do with your win. Sadly, many slot players will give her a tip for her tip.

Many casinos have now told their slot employees to keep their mouths shut about hot machines since the slot executives are well aware there is no such thing as a predictably hot machine. The machines are unpredictable, and that is the truth. Yet, payouts with some small bills and with longstanding attendants looking adoringly into your eyes are things that no executive can stop.

Perhaps the worst practitioners of tip hustling ply their trade at the strictly slots joints where workers get much of their income from luring in customers who then give them tips should their machines hit. You can hear them barking at people walking by on the street, "Hey, come on in, I know a machine that is about to hit! You might get rich." P.T. Barnum was right, of course, and to paraphrase: In the gambling world, there is a sucker born every minute.

Are the antics of these slot workers illegal? Are their antics immoral?

I'd guess these tactics are not illegal since, as far as I know, over many decades no law-enforcement agency has arrested any of the practitioners. Are these tactics immoral? I don't know. Taking advantage of people's hopes and desires is a long tradition in business. You want whiter floors? Buy this product. The product may or may not make your floors whiter, but that's the hope of the buyer and the promise of the seller.

At craps games you will see the same hustling of hopes (or is that dopes?) as the stick person encourages players to make the worst bets on the table, known as the Crazy Crapper bets. And boy do the craps players charge in to make such terrible bets.

I guess the tip-hustling motto should be "caveat emptor"—which, translated into gambling parlance, means, "Let winning players beware!"

The bottom line of casino gambling is simple to write: In random games, no one can accurately predict what is going to occur. No betting scheme, no slot attendant, no slot hustler at the slot parlors, no stick person at craps, no *anyone* can say what will or will not happen; what or who will or will not get hot or where all these unknowns are destined to happen. Your astrology charts can pick out lucky numbers, lucky days, and lucky colors; there is no greater proof of astrology's ability to make correct predictions than the fawning attendant saying in a hushed tone, "That's the hot machine over there. It's about to hit."

So why do so many otherwise intelligent people fall for such nonsense? Perhaps this will answer the question: When Pandora opened the box of evils, only one thing remained inside—hope. I guess inside every casino gambler is the hope that even though these games can't really be beaten, somehow they have reached inside Pandora's Box and snatched out the only thing to hold onto.

Should you tip a slot attendant? Come on!

CHAPTER 12

The Total Slot Experience

I've heard them, you've heard them: "I played for 36 straight hours, and I was so bleary-eyed I couldn't even tell if I won after a while. I got home from Vegas, and I had to sleep for two days to recover. I didn't do anything but play those machines! I lost all the money I brought to play with, and boy did I have fun...I think."

Some people might think, *Wow! What a great vacation Sally must have had!*

But did she really? Well, of course she might think so, but, in fact, what did she really do? Not much. She stayed up all hours, became bleary-eyed, and, uh, that was it. She could have done that at home without losing any money.

The fact is that some casino players have been trained, or have trained themselves, or have been acculturated into a system that prizes mindlessness as some form of merit. Seriously, going to Las Vegas to just play slot machines and do nothing else? Ridiculous! You want to do that kind of silly thing, then you can play for unending losing hours on the Internet.

Most of you have seen such players staying up all odd hours, playing endlessly, half asleep or half awake, groggy, perhaps blitzed, sometimes incoherent and semicomatose, as if pushing the envelope of endurance is some badge of honor as opposed to an act of extreme silliness. Perhaps you have done this yourself.

I remember a befuddled woman the beautiful AP and I met on April 2 at the Golden Nugget in Las Vegas. She had a drink in her hand, and she asked me what time it was. I told her the time. The she asked, "Its April 1, right?" When I told her that it was April 2, she asked me where April 1 went. She had played so long she had lost track of the days!

I am guessing she had no idea of how much money she played in all that time or how much she had lost or, a long shot, how much she might be ahead. The whole slot-playing experience to her was merely a dream. She probably said what many vacationers have said after particularly grueling vacations: "I need a vacation from my vacation!"

Now think of this. If you go to Las Vegas, just wrap your mind around the fact that Vegas has some of the best restaurants on Earth, some of the best shopping, many of the best shows, and some of the best sightseeing in the whole nation—both natural and manmade. The Strip itself at all hours of the day and night is a visual treat and a lesson in watching examples of humanity from all over the world.

Juxtapose that with sitting at a slot machine for 36 straight hours, bleary-eyed, and then returning home to brag about your vacation and the fact that what you accomplished was losing your gambling money. Again, a ridiculous waste of time!

Now I am not saying that you shouldn't gamble when you go to Vegas—after all, Vegas is still the gambling capital of the planet—but gambling is only one of so many things you can experience, that to restrict yourself solely to this activity is, well, *ridiculous*. When you travel, when you vacation, when you leave the confines of your normal day-to-day existence, the joy should be in multiple experiences, not a singular draining one.

At the end of your life's days, when you are summing up your life and your memories, sitting on your butt for 36 hours is probably not going to be one of your most memorable experiences. In fact, it might not become a memory at all.

But if you attend any of the Cirque du Soleil shows, you will experience jaw-dropping, truly mind-boggling entertainment that will leave you saying, "How can they do those things?"

Go to any of the other regular superstar shows or those Broadway musicals now making the Vegas rounds, and you are in for a great experience. There are also loads of comedy shows, adult-themed shows (meaning *va-va-va-voom!*) for both men and women, and free afternoon entertainment in many casinos. Just walking the Strip offers some fabulous sights: the volcano in front of the Mirage, the Sirens of Titan epic in front of TI (Treasure Island), and the fountains at Bellagio, to name three.

And great days and evenings are not limited to Las Vegas, either. Atlantic City has the Atlantic Ocean and great restaurants, shopping, and shows as well. There is not a casino venue in the country that doesn't offer something else besides endless gambling.

There is so much to enjoy in the casino world that to miss out on these other things is, again, ridiculous.

Keeping Your Rhythm

You are having some fun outside the slot aisles, but how should you structure your playing day when you are face-to-face with those sparkling, tempting slot machines?

The greatest casino player I ever knew was the Captain, an Atlantic City legend. The Captain was not a slot player but the consummate craps player who nevertheless taught me so much about casino gambling that it changed my whole philosophy about how to approach all the games, including slots.

I have written several books and a DVD about the Captain's methods of play, the latest being *Casino Craps: Shoot to Win!* and *Cutting Edge Craps: Advanced Strategies for Serious Players!* and I firmly believe that all players—table-game players *and* slot players—can benefit from his insights and recommendations. It doesn't matter what games you play. The Captain's advice applies to all of them and to any trip you make to the casino-hotels.

The Captain was a firm believer that casino players often get themselves into big economic trouble by disrupting their normal daily rhythms to imitate or duplicate the 24/7 rhythm of the casino. This is a dangerous thing, both physically and mentally, because it makes rational thinking quite hard, if not impossible.

The Captain believed that you must impose your normal, daily rhythm when you go to the casinos for a stay of whatever length. You must not allow the 24/7 rhythm of the casino to dominate you.

Get up in the morning at the same time you normally do, have breakfast at the same time that you normally do, shower or bathe at the same time you normally do—then go to work, meaning, play a session at the machines. Break for lunch at the normal time. Then you can play another session or do something else, such as go swimming or shopping, take a nap, or go out to dinner. After dinner, play another session or go to a show and then go to sleep about the same time as you go to sleep every night when you are home.

The Captain believed that if you keep as close to a normal daily schedule as possible, your mind will stay clear and you will have a much smaller chance of falling prey to poor judgments because you haven't been thrown off your normal rhythm.

Most slot players have to ask themselves the question of whether playing for endless hours is really all that much fun or if it is more like an induced state of mesmerism. Do you really have as much fun in the 10th straight hour of play as you have in the second hour of play? My guess, for most players, anyway, is that the 10th hour passes by in a haze.

In truth, what makes slot playing so much fun for most players is the anticipatory nature of the game. You tend to have losing streaks of various durations, all the while building your adrenaline for the big rush during a hoped-for big hit. This is the joy of slot playing, anticipation, but that joy is almost completely blunted when you are somewhat "out of it." That "out of it" can be caused by lack of sleep or too much to drink or a combination of both.

The Captain believed it is actually more fun to play when you are fully cognizant of what is happening. In short, your "now" of playing is more fun, and your memory of "past" play, once you return home, will be clearer. In short, you'll remember your casino adventures better!

I am fully aware that some casino players think that a necessary ingredient of going to the casinos is for the player to lose control. They view their casino time as some kind of "letting it all hang out" experience. According to the Captain, not only is that dangerous to your health, it is also dangerous to your bankroll and your peace of mind.

The ploppy fools can "let it all hang out," but you be wise—follow the Captain's advice. You'll be glad you did.

More on the Rhythm Method: Cruise Control

The first time I ever used my "cruise control" on my new car disoriented me to some degree. I had to get used to the road without my foot on the gas pedal. Strange as it might seem, the feel of the road is entirely different when you drive using your car's cruise control. It took a little while to get used to it, but now when I can use it, well, it's the only way to go. Cruise control rules!

I am less tired on a long drive (which means a 146-mile drive to Atlantic City or the 186-mile drive to my favorite hideaway, Cape May in New Jersey). Cruise control relieves a lot of stress for me because I am a person who really doesn't relish driving. In fact, I drive about five miles a week in my real life, while my wife drives about 40 miles per week. We had a 1995 car that I gave to my son in early 2008 that only had 60,000 miles on it.

So cruise control makes driving a heck of a lot easier for me. Set the miles per hour, and that's that. The car doesn't go faster; it doesn't go slower. You can stay within the speed limit and not get caught up in the mad rush of maniacal ploppies who feel it is their duty to go 10 to 20 mph faster than the law allows.

Of course, cruise control can have a slight problem. There could be a tendency for your mind to drift off and not be as aware of what you are doing. You then drive the same speed, but your mind is breaking. Not a good thing at all.

Playing slots is like driving on a highway. Players usually start off at a reasonable speed and then, as time passes (and/or as comped drinks are consumed), their speed picks up until they are going over their speed limit—which is their wallets' or purses' ability to withstand the type of bad sessions one can have playing so many decisions. Too fast is too bad at gambling games. That's a fact that can't be disputed.

The typical tendency of the majority of slot players is to increase the pressure on the gas pedal as they play for longer and longer time periods. Playing longer and longer generally translates into playing faster and faster with more decisions per hour and more decisions in total. It's a formula for losses you might not be prepared for.

So what is the solution to this? Use a slot-playing type of cruise control.

There is absolutely no reason why you must play faster and faster the longer and longer you play. It's a habit formation, much like the habits of the ploppies who career wildly, risking life and limb, on the highways and byways of America.

So how do you incorporate a cruise control into your slot play? Well, it will take some modicum of discipline.

You can do it one of two ways. Simply reduce the number of spins you do in a minute. (Okay, I have said this before, but it bears repeating here.) If you do 12 spins now, go down to 10 or seven, or take the leap and go down to five. That saves a ton off your potential losses. However, do not play longer because you have reduced your minute-by-minute bankroll hit.

Of course, counting the time or number of spins can be a really dull or even torturous activity and might even take away from the fun of trying to break those one-armed bandits. So if you don't want to do that, here is another way to reduce your slot-playing mileage.

The second way to use slot-playing cruise control, and perhaps the easiest way, is simply to take a 10-minute break every hour of play. If you normally go an hour straight, go for 25 minutes, take a five-minute break to walk around, then go play another 25 minutes, then take another five-minute break. Continue to play your normal number of hours in a given day, but you will have reduced the hit on your money by about 17 percent.

If you intend to make slot playing your preferred method of attempting to relieve the casinos of their cash, then you better put the breaks on your slot-car somewhat. You don't want to wind up like those slot players who have quit because, as one told me, "What's the use? I keep getting my head handed to me."

Put that cruise control on, and drive those slot machines a little slower. Your bankroll will be able to last a lot longer, and you'll be able to enjoy the trip much more than if you uncontrollably careened down those slot aisles like those ploppies do on the roads.

Words to the wise.

CHAPTER 13

Playing Slots Every Day

I received a letter from a man who wished to play craps every day and wanted to know how much he would need in a total bankroll and what his monetary expectation would be. Then it hit me: what kind of bankroll would you need to play *slots* every day for one year? Of course, the slot question is a tough one, because there are all sorts of machines out there with all sorts of paybacks. One could also say there are all sorts of craps bets too, but my correspondent had only two specific bets in mind, so it made judging what he needed to play and how much he would lose fairly straightforward.

So let's take two typical slot players—one a 25¢ player and one a $1 player. Each will play three coins in the machines every day for one year using four hours a day as the playing time. Let's figure 12 spins per minute, with 720 spins per hour, with 2,880 spins per day, with a total of 1,051,200 spins in one year.

Let's say the 25¢ machine has a generous payback of about 91 percent in this scenario. That means the house edge is 9 percent. The total losing expectation for 75¢ play will be $48.60 per hour in losses, with $194.40 in losses per day and with $70,956 in losses per year.

On the $1 machines we can say that the payback is about 92 percent, and therefore the house edge is 8 percent. Our $1 player loses $172.80 per hour, $691 in losses per day, and $252,288 in losses per year.

Looking at these figures, I would speculate that very few players would have the resources to take a $70,956 loss at a quarter machine, and unless they were one of the few megamillionaires, swallowing that gargantuan $252,288 loss on dollar slots would be out of the question.

So how can you reduce these losses and still play every day in a single year? Here is a list of what you can do.

1. Play six spins per minute, not 12.
2. Play one coin, not three.

With six spins per minute, you will face 360 spins per hour at 25¢ each. That means you will put in $90 per hour with an expected loss of $8.10 per hour, $32.40 per day, and $11,826 per year. That yearly expected loss is a lot better than $70,956, isn't it?

For the dollar player, the drop in expected losses is just as dramatic. At 360 spins at $1 each, the player puts through $360 per hour with an expected loss of $28.80. For one day the dollar player's expectation is a loss of $115.30, and for one year the expected loss will be $42,048.

For all slot players, that six-spins-per-minute rule seems to be a hard thing to do because, as slot players get into the groove of playing, they play faster and faster—unfortunately for them and fortunately for the casinos. The more decisions a slot player faces, the worse it is for him; the more decisions a casino faces, the better it is for the casino.

In short, whoever has the edge at a game realizes that edge with increasing numbers of decisions. Advantage-slot players want to play fast; all other slot players must play as slow as their mental and emotional constitution allows.

Is it really that hard to make a conscious effort to spin those reels every 10 seconds, which is what six spins per minute comes to? I think with knowledge of what you want to do when you are playing can keep that house edge somewhat at bay by keeping the number of decisions low. Make a conscious effort to do this.

You have to play just one coin too. As I have clearly shown, the jackpots on regular machines will not push up the return enough to make it worthwhile to play maximum coin. I explained this when I wrote about money management. Slot machines are not video-poker machines where max coin is a must. It is just the opposite for most slot machines.

And while we're speaking about rules for play, once again my advice is to avoid those giant progressives, as the house edge is about 15 to 17 percent; avoid the mega-multiline nickel machines; get your play into the 25¢–$1 range on traditional machines and not the mega-nickel ones. Those nickel machines and now those penny machines often have extremely high house edges, and you are putting in nearly the same amount of money as you would be on the standard 25¢ and $1 machines, which are far looser.

You can go even further and do four or five spins a minute and reduce your expected losses even more. As you can see, the losses are rather high even with my cost-saving strategies. Is it any wonder the casinos win a fortune from the slot machines? A single person will probably never play every day, but the combined play of all slot players takes place every second of every minute of every day.

Many slot players have a vague idea of the kind of hit the house edge puts on their bankroll, but only a small percentage have worked out the actual math. Once you do, you have to realize that less is best. When it comes to playing those machines, you have to use moderation, or you'll be immoderately hammered.

CHAPTER 14
Slots *Un*-Etiquette

She's hovering behind you, leaning over so you can smell her garlicky breath and hear her tortured breathing from too much smoking over the course of a lifetime. You are tormented by her never-ending raspy commentary on each and every spin of the reels. She isn't playing, but she has hitched a ride on your star. "Oh, you almost had a good one that time. Look above your pay line, my friend, and you can see the symbols you almost got. Keep going, and you might hit something. This might be a lucky machine. Can't wait to see you get something. Let's hang in there and see what happens, honey."

Why doesn't she just go away, buzz off, and leave you alone? Joining a slot player while he or she plays is totally discourteous, and I have seen this happen quite a bit in some casinos, especially those that cater to local players or the bus crowd. Playing slots is not an excuse to barge into someone else's playing space.

* * *

He comes over holding his beer, somewhat tipsy and with food stains on his shirt and dribble on his chin, and he slurs, "How haf yo bean doin, buddsy? Win any mommy yet? How muff is if?" You want to ask him to move along and not foul your air with his beer breathing, but you know this could lead to a confrontation. So you hold your breath for as long as possible. Finally you get up and go. If God is with you, the wobbly drunken slob doesn't follow you. If he does follow you, then, men, you should go to the bathroom and not leave until he has left. Stay in the stall. Hopefully you won't have to camp out. If you are a woman, also go to the bathroom. Chances are he'll stagger away, as even most drunks know not to go into the ladies' room (I hope).

* * *

She ambles over slowly, carrying an oversized pocketbook that looks more like a suitcase stuffed with bowling balls or the heads of slot players she's recently decapitated. She then aggressively informs you, "You know I come here all the time, and I have never seen you here. Everyone knows this is *my* machine. Everyone in this whole casino knows me. Could you go to another machine? I like this machine. You can ask anyone here that I come here all the time. I consider that *my* machine. I have given this casino enough money that they should name this machine after me."

She now puts down that huge bag and waits for you to get up and leave *her* machine. She starts to twirl her orange hair (or she might even have that strange blue hair many elderly women have), and you can swear she is tapping her swollen feet. You don't know what to do with her staring at you with those beady laser eyes. If you have been lucky on the machine, the decision could be difficult. If the machine is in an advantage-play mode because it is an advantage-play machine in a player-friendly mode, then you will just have to put up with her grousing. You might just say to her when you are on an advantage-play machine, "I'll be through in a little while." Or you could tell her the brutal truth: "Listen, you battle axe. I am not leaving the machine until it hits the jackpot, so you might have a long wait."

* * *

"Hold up," he says to you. "I'm playing *all* these machines, each machine in this whole row, you understand? Look up and down the row, these are all mine...mine, you hear me?" When you tell him that he hasn't played any of the other machines since you came over, he responds harshly, "Who are you, the slot police? I play them in a special supersecret sequence, and the supersecret sequence hasn't called for me to bet any of the other machines in this row yet, got that? So all those machines belong to me, or I can't do the supersecret sequence, understand?"

You really want to tell him that his supersecret slot sequence is nonsense and that he'll lose money in the long run on all those machines no matter what he does. But, being polite, you slowly walk away. The casino is getting crowded, and you wonder if the powers that be will let him continue to hog a whole row of machines. You guess that if this guy is a big long-term loser on high-denomination machines, the casino will probably not say a thing. He's the Thanksgiving turkey to be gutted, cooked, and eaten by the house.

* * *

She pushes herself up and goes right into your face when you tell her this machine was saved for you. She clearly sees the card that says *Reserved* on the machine. Her massive jowls shake with anger, her face balloons up in a pulsating red color, then she belligerently shouts, "I don't care that the dumb slot worker said she would reserve this machine while you went to the bathroom. You weren't here, so the machine belongs to me. Go away." She throws the *Reserved* sign at you and plops her jiggling jelly butt into the chair. "Get lost!"

Now what do you do? The slot attendant can verify she had saved your machine for you, but that attendant has no real power, and is a confrontation with this massively insane individual worth ruining your day? You and the slot attendant look at each other, roll your eyes, and then you head for greener pastures, hoping she doesn't have a bigger sister waiting for you at another machine.

* * *

"So what do you do for a living?" she asks as she gently sits herself on the seat next to you, an overperfumed, stretch-faced, chicken-necked woman who wishes to recapture some youth and merely looks foolish and sad. "I'm a retired language teacher, and I love to come to the casinos. It's such a social place, don't you think? Do you come here very much? This isn't such a hot casino in my opinion."

She continues, "I'm here with my husband, who is over there getting sloshed. The machines are always cold here. I don't think I ever saw anyone win anything on a machine in this place. My favorite casinos are in Vegas, which is the best place to go to play. Have you ever been there? You should try it some time. Makes this place look like a cheesy dump, and I can't figure who would ever want to play here except my inebriated husband...." And on it goes, nonstop.

When you run into a talker, even a pleasant one, the endless stream of words causes you to think she is a talking, walking dictionary. The only thing you can do is get up or try to ignore her—which is a hard thing to do. Pleasant talkers can be as big a pain in the machine as nasty ones.

* * *

He is furious. "I was about to play that machine when you jumped in here and hit my jackpot. Don't you realize that was my jackpot because I was about to play the machine?" How do you handle this? You can say, "The RNG doesn't know you were going to play. Each split second a different random number is played, and had you sat down, you wouldn't have gotten the jackpot because the machine would have been played at a different moment." Since he probably won't understand what you're talking about, you can say instead, "That's happened to me many times. Sometimes you just have bad luck and someone else takes the jackpot. Sorry about that."

* * *

He snorts his bulbous nose as he passes by you with his loud, laughing friends. He pontificates at the top of his squeaky voice, "Playing slots is the dumbest thing in the whole casino. These people here," he sweeps his hand to include all slot players in the casino including you, "are all idiots; total, complete idiots. I'm a blackjack player. Now there's a game that can be beaten, sometimes, if you know what you are doing. But no one has ever won on the slots, so why do these suckers play these stupid machines? What the heck is wrong with these people? There's an idiot born every second." Thankfully he and his pontifical posse just pass you by.

* * *

"Want to know how to win on the slots?" he asks. "There's a great slots system that I am selling to special people, and I can tell you are a special person just by looking at you. And you can buy it right now, and here is what I can do for you. I sell you this system, but it is free; no money down, nothing like that at all. I mean it is completely free. You play the system right with me next to you, and whatever you win we split 50–50. How does that sound to you? You risk nothing using the winning system I am giving you for free, and we get to take home some good money. What do you think? It's a good deal. You can't lose with it, can you?"

There it is; some of the *un*-etiquette of the slot world. The key to each of these incidents is the fact that some people will take it upon themselves to annoy you. It doesn't happen at slots as much as it does at blackjack, but it still does occasionally happen. Often the best way to handle such annoyances is to get up and go to another machine (unless you are playing advantage machines in a positive mode). *Flight* in such cases is a much better response than *fight*.

CHAPTER 15

The Great Myths of Slots

ove over, you monsters. Yes, Bigfoot, the Loch Ness Monster, those bug-eyed aliens, and the Abominable Snowman are merely minor real-world myths that can't hold an RNG to the myriad reel-world myths that have developed about slot machines. Some of the slot-machine myths are based on a kind of logic (wrong conclusions logically derived from wrong premises), and some are totally whacked out, seemingly coming from the tortured minds of maniacal madmen and weird women. Here are a slew of the myths coupled with their truths, to disabuse any of you who are true believers in this falseness.

The Myth: *There will be no more jackpots after a big one has been hit so the machine can make sure it meets its payback percentage.*
The Truth: The hitting of the jackpot is not determined by a recent hitting of the jackpot. The machine does not say to itself, "Oh, that player just hit a jackpot, better stop all future jackpots until I make back the money!" The statistics of the machine include jackpot hits, and should randomness hit a second jackpot right after another jackpot, that is no big deal. The reason people think the machines tighten up after a jackpot is simple: jackpots are long shots, and hitting them in close succession is highly improbable, yes, but not impossible.

The Myth: *Older slot machines are much tighter than newer machines because players in the past were far stupider than players are today.*
The Truth: The old Las Vegas probably had looser machines than it does today because it was far less expensive to operate a casino in those days. Table games brought in so much more money that casinos didn't have to worry about charging for rooms and meals. Comps were far more generous. Were players stupider then than they are now? I doubt that too. The casinos cater to a wide range of human intelligence, from ploppies to geniuses. It just seems like many of the players are stupid because of the gambling decisions that they make.

The Myth: *Slot-machine symbols each have an equal chance of being hit.*
The Truth: No. The RNG determines what comes up, and the symbols do not have an equal chance of coming up; some come up more, and some come up less.

The Myth: *Someone just hit a jackpot on the machine you just left. If you stayed, you would hit that jackpot instead of that rat who replaced you.*
The Truth: Since the RNG is working in the tenths of seconds, where it picks this or that sequence of numbers, which relate to the symbols you see, even a split-second difference in hitting the play button between you and that rodent will change what combinations come up. So between you getting up and that rat sitting down, the RNG has gone through thousands of symbols. In short, the rat didn't steal your cheese.

The Myth: *Like follows like or the opposite. If you are using a machine that still takes coins, heat your coins up with a lighter, and the machine will start to pay off because the heat in the coins will generate heat in the machine. If you use cold coins, the machine will warm up to get it back to its correct temperature, and the only way to do this is to hit jackpots because the friction of the credit spins causes small amounts of heat.*
The Truth: The person who came up with these methods is now resting comfortably in a local mental ward. Obviously, these ideas are crazy. I recall one gentleman in Atlantic City who tried to light a coin with a

lighter, and the coin got so hot his skin stuck to it and he had to be taken to the hospital by the EMTs.

The Myth: *Casinos can loosen or tighten the slot machines by flipping a switch, which is either inside the cover or in back of the machine. If you can locate the switch in the back, you can make the machine get much hotter.*
The Truth: Slot machines work on computer chips, and these chips are put in the machines at the factory. They are expensive to replace and require all sorts of paperwork in most jurisdictions to do this. So it isn't just flipping a switch. When slot-machine companies sell their products to casinos, they offer the casinos various payback percentages, and the casinos pick which ones they want.

The Myth: *Slot machines are programmed by a computer to go through cycles of wins and losses. Once the computer goes through the cycle it will repeat itself. This is an opportunity to beat the machine by following the cycles as they are played.*
The Truth: The machines are random, and each spin is independent of the last spin. Much like a flipped coin being 50/50, you still can't predict which will be flipped next because the flip is a random event. But over a sufficiently long period of time you will start to see the results coming closer and closer to 50/50.

The Myth: *The casino has you hooked once you start using a player's club card. You put that card in the machine, and it tightens up the payouts. Why? Because the casino knows you are a sucker for using their card, so why give a sucker an even break?*
The Truth: The computer inside the machine doesn't distinguish between those who use player's cards from those players who don't use such cards. The RNG that picks the symbols is not connected to the player's-club-card component of the machine. All you do if you believe this myth is limit the comps the casino will give you for playing. In short, you are losing even more money because you are not getting comped returns on your play. So the bottom line is that the odds of winning and losing on the

machine are the same whether you use a player's club card or whether you don't.

The Myth: *The IRS is everywhere hunting people down to take their money. If you use a player's club card, the IRS is sent all the information about how much you've won on the machines. That is the prime reason not to use a player's club card when you play the machines.*

The Truth: The slot club card doesn't report anything to the IRS. However, if you win $1,200 or more in a single spin, then the casino will report that amount to the IRS. It doesn't matter whether you used a player's card or not. Now, the casino does not report smaller wins to the government agency. Players must do this themselves, and I am sure there must be a couple of players out there who would actually do such a thing. By the way, in some countries gambling wins are not taxable. It used to be this way in the United States, but no more.

The Myth: *More jackpots are won during the week than are won on weekends in order to get people to play when the casinos aren't that crowded.*

The Truth: It's hospital time again! The player who came up with this idea is in the room next to the person who came up with the hot-coin/cold-coin strategy. First, it makes no sense. If you could muck around with jackpots, why bother doing it midweek to encourage small groups of players to play when doing this on a weekend would encourage a much, much larger group of players to play? But never mind logic. This just isn't so. Indeed, more jackpots are hit on weekends than on the weekdays of Monday through Thursday for one reason and one reason only: more players are playing on the weekends. Thus more decisions are being made, and with more decisions there is a greater likelihood of some jackpots being hit somewhere in the casino. It's all in the long-run statistics.

The Myth: *The more I play a machine, the more likely I am to win.*

The Truth: Just the opposite. This myth only looks at the idea that with more decisions being played, the better the player's chances for hitting a jackpot. This is true—to an extent. Keep in mind that each individual decision is random. Yes, the statistics of the game show how often a jackpot is supposed to hit, but those statistics can't tell us when the jackpot will hit. Unfortunately, with more decisions, the more the house edge is grinding and hammering away at your money. While doing hundreds of thousands of spins might allow you to hit a jackpot, the fact is that your overall losses will probably not be changed by such a hit. This fact is inescapable: the longer you play, the better the chance that you will be behind. The longer you play, the better the chance that the casino will be ahead—whether you hit a jackpot or not. The only exception to this rule is the advantage-play slot machines where the more you play the better your chances of being ahead.

The Myth: *Aren't there such things as "holiday machines" that the casinos bring in to rip people off during Christmas and other holidays?*
The Truth: These would be the "Un-Merry Christmas" machines? They don't exist. Scrooge machines are just myths, as "weekend dice" are myths of the craps world.

The Myth: *I know a person* (Please add in the person being referred to: my mother-in-law, my friend, a guy in my club, the person who cleans my house, a person I hang with on the beach, a person I bowl with, a fellow drinker and drug user, the girls in my sewing circle, the boys in my knitting class, the cook at Munch's Restaurant and Dry Cleaners, the steroidal monstrosity at my local gym) *who never loses on the machines. He has a set plan and when he loses several spins on one machine, he gets up and goes to another machine. One of the new machines eventually gets hot, and then he wins his money. If he loses a set amount on quarter machines, he will then go up to $1 machines, and he even goes to $5 machines. He has never lost in a trip to the casinos.*
The Truth: There is a reasonable chance that on one, two, or several successive trips to the casinos, a person can come home a winner regardless of how he plays. Except for persons playing advantage-play machines, those playing the normal slots will have a greater and greater chance to be losers the more and more often they play. Now, if this person "who never loses" has been playing for a long, long time, he is not coming home a winner on every trip. If he says he is, he is a liar. I think the myth of the "person who never loses" gives hope to many slot players that there is a chance of being ahead on the negative-expectation machines by simply

using interesting strategies that actually have nothing to do with being able to beat such a random game where the house has an edge. Indeed, hope springs eternal in the breasts of the slot-playing public. Other than on advantage-play machines, is it possible for a player to be ahead for his or her slot-playing career? Yes, it's a dim—a very, very dim—possibility. Those who have hit a monstrous jackpot on those progressive machines such as Megabucks can finish their slot-playing lives ahead of the house. But such winners are a fraction of a fraction of a fraction of a percent. I am pretty sure these winners won't include you or me.

The Myth: *New slot machines with mega-multiline wins and great graphics and cartoons that do fun things when you win something are looser than the traditional machines in order to get the players to play the new machines.*
The Truth: I don't know with certainty here, but logic would say that the more time the machine takes up with nonplay entertainment, no money is being made for the casino during those times. Therefore the machines might be tighter to make up for the down time of the nonplay entertainment features. Or you get fewer comp points for playing such a machine.

The Myth: *More winning combinations are hit when a player plays maximum coins on a machine.*
The Truth: Only on "Buy a Pay" or "Buy a Play" machines will this myth actually be true. On all other machines, the RNG will not distinguish between one coin, two coins, or whatever is maximum coin.

The Myth: *On traditional slots, pulling the handle makes the machine looser because so few players pull it. Most players prefer to hit the play button which then makes the machine tighter.*
The Truth: Not so. The RNG does not distinguish the handle pull from the play button. Indeed, if you play slots with handle pulls, you will probably be playing fewer decisions. In such a case, your overall expectation will be "less bad" than someone constantly hitting the play button.

CHAPTER 16

Let Your Voices Be Heard

I know about the programming of slots, as I've done some consulting work for slot manufacturers. And, yes, I know about the RNG. And I certainly know what a payback percentage means and how those various payback percentages translate into house edges on the various machines.

Yes, I also know what areas of the country have the best slot paybacks on various denominations and what areas have the lowest returns on the various machines. In some venues, such as Atlantic City, I even know what the paybacks are at distinct casinos.

Okay, so what didn't I know about the slot machines?

In just about every issue of the magazine *Strictly Slots*, Frank Legato, a funny and insightful slot writer, describes many of the new and sometimes old machines. He explains how they are played and usually what manufacturers have made the machines. Then he informs us as to what locations have already booked these machines (or are about to book them).

That's not the revelation. All gambling writers know these facts.

What grabbed my attention when I was last reading Frank's column on the new machines was a single line that said, "Payback % Range." Under this Legato gave the manufacturers' range of paybacks. That's when I had my revelation!

I have read this line and the line under this line for years, and it never dawned on me that it shouldn't be the casinos' choice as to what payback they have on these machines—it should be *you* and all slot players all over the country!

If new machines are hitting the floors, why shouldn't they be the variety with the highest payback? That's what I would like to see, and I am sure that's what you would like to see. Why would any slot player want to see anything else?

Let's take a look at one machine of the hundreds that Frank has written about to get some idea of what I am talking about. The name of the machine is "Anything But Six" created by International Game Technology. That machine may not be on the slot floors anymore, but that is irrelevant. It is the following thought that counts.

The Payback % Range goes from 85 percent to 98 percent. That's a monstrous 15 percent house edge down to a mere 2 percent house edge. What do the outer edges of this payback mean in terms of your money? Well, at the 85 percent range, for every $100 you wager in the machine, your expectation is to lose $15. While the 98 percent machine is expected to lose you a mere (meaning tiny, measly, and relatively small) $2 for every $100 you wager. That is some great difference, isn't it?

So what can you, the slot players, do about this? You must write letters to the casinos where new machines are being installed asking, demanding, pleading with the casino to only install the highest percentage payback that the machine allows.

Yes, I'll admit, a few letters might not sway the slot-machine directors to make their machines as loose as they can possibly be—but thousands of letters might have a positive effect. I am hoping this book can generate those thousands of letters—no, make that hundreds of thousands of letters (which means this book is selling like a California wildfire).

Here is a sample letter that you can use—adapt as you see fit:

Dear [Name of Slot Director]:

It has come to my attention that you have the [name of slot machine] as a part of your inventory or that you are planning to have that machine as a part of your inventory. According to Frank Legato of Strictly Slots *magazine, the range of possible paybacks is [give "Payback % Range"].*

I am asking you to please use the highest possible payback on that machine.

I think you will find that with more wins, the players will in fact play longer at the machines, be more satisfied with their play, and keep coming back for more because they are getting a good deal at your casino. You can even advertise that you are giving the highest payback possible on these machines, and that will make players know that you are giving them the best machine possible.

I really hope you follow my suggestion and let me know. If you do, I will be there to play as a loyal customer and bring my entire family!

Yours truly,

Your Name

Okay, this is something new and unheard of. You, the citizens of the slot-machine world, can now rise up and ask for what you want—the best payouts on the machines!

And that is why I am a dolt, because I never realized what this information could be used for. Slot players must stand up and let their voices be heard.

CHAPTER 17

Slot Scammers
and Other Creeps

T hey crawl from beneath the dusty floorboards of deceit with sharpened fangs, ready to bite into the necks of innocent slot players who are looking to realize their dreams of big and even bigger wins. These horrid moldy creatures are the slot scammers, looking to relieve players of their money by promising them untold riches at the machines. Short of a lightning strike on one of those awful linked progressives, "untold riches" at slot machines aren't in the reels for almost all of us.

Yet, slot scammers know something that some slot players don't know or have not yet learned or sadly will never learn, and it is this: slot players are a hopeful lot and will often throw their money away on a promise that sells a dream of riches. The scammers know this full well and literally bank on it.

There are a number of slot scams that are beautiful in their simplicity and deviousness, and these scams reel in the slot players as if they are hungry fish fascinated by a colorful metal lure. I know of these scams because in the early years of my casino-gambling career, I fell for most of them myself. Oh, yes, I confess that in my careless youth I was always looking for the magic gambling bullet until I realized that hard work and knowledge were those bullets. As best-selling gaming author Bill Burton writes, "Luck comes and goes, but knowledge lasts forever."

91

So what should you look for in the typical slots scam? First, the advertisement you are reading will be overly long. The seller will hammer you over and over again about the amazing benefits of his product. There will be a host of testimonials from phony sources telling you that they have won thousands, tens of thousands, hundreds of thousands, and the really brazen ones will state they have won millions. The seller will also claim that he has won outrageous amounts and is now retired and living on an island or in a mansion in the beautiful mountains (wherever in the world there are beautiful mountains) or in France or wherever he thinks you'll think is a great place to live on your slot winnings.

He'll explain that he is only offering this incredible deal for a short period of time and that you had better get on it right away. This is, of course, the typical sales pitch used by legitimate businesses and scammers alike. Make the potential buyer feel rushed to buy because time is running out on this great offer. Naturally the seller will promise you your money back if his system doesn't work. Will you get your money back when his system invariably doesn't work? Can pigs fly?

After the *War and Peace*-length advertisement, the seller will now state his price and usually offer another product for free if you hurry and buy before the deadline.

Interestingly enough, some years ago a scammer photocopied pages of an early book of mine, along with some of my slot articles, removed my name (naturally), and then sold these ideas as foolproof ways to win. They weren't foolproof (have you ever tried to proof something against a fool?), and I never wrote that they were foolproof. But what did he care? He sold these photocopies for $99 until my team of lawyers nailed his buttocks to the wall. My understanding is that this scammer then photocopied some other author's ideas, removed that author's name, and sold this foolproof system for $39.

Except for the advantage-play machines in this book, there is no way to get an edge on the slot machines. You know that, and I know that the house programs the machines to win itself money, which means that you lose your money, a fact of slot-play life. But scammers can't make money from you unless they can convince you that they have come up with a secret formula that will assure you of big wins. One fun way to do that is to show all the 1099 forms the seller has won over the years of playing his system. As you know, if you play the slots a lot, those 1099s can really add up even as your losses are adding up with them.

They run a delicatessen of deceit about themselves and their rancid systems. Oh, by the way, the overwhelming majority of these scammers are men, and the majority of the buyers of these systems are also men. Go figure. The systems come in various guises of the same idea. I am paraphrasing the bologna from the scammers.

- I can show you when the machines will be hot.
- I can show you what machines to avoid because they are getting cold.
- I can show you the trick slot pros use to win millions.
- I can show you a money-management system guaranteed to make you win.
- I can tell you what slot machines are money producers and which aren't.
- I have a PhD in physics and can tell when machines will pay out.
- I am an engineer and have looked inside the machines to discover their secrets to paying out large sums to smart players such as you.
- My system is based on an age-old forgotten understanding of how real probability really works in the real world of real slot playing.
- Using this technique has won me millions of dollars, and I have the 1099 forms to prove my wins over the casinos.
- I live on a tropical island where beautiful women cater to my every need.
- I live on a tropical island where I do nothing but lounge on the beach all day and think of all the money I have taken from the casinos.
- I am giving you this foolproof system to share my knowledge of how to beat the house and win millions.
- Everything I am doing is based on the latest cutting-edge science that no one knows about except a few of us.
- My mentor, Doctor Yaba-Daba-Do, has revealed his decades-long study of how the slots really work, and I am his student willing to share everything he has taught me.

- Let me explain how to play the machines to assure that you'll win the big jackpots and not just small change.
- I will give you your money back if you don't win; you can trust me on that.
- I have never had to give money back because my clients always win.
- I have never had a losing trip to the casinos.
- My supersecret device will find hot machines in the blink of an eye.

The "due" theory of slot play is the typical system the scammers sell, because such systems rely on the gambler's mistaken notion of predictable trends in random games. Of course there are no predictable trends in a random game, but most gamblers just can't wrap their minds around this idea. It violates their sense that all things come in foreseeable patterns.

My "favorite" evil scam is one that has been used in all casino games. The seller offers you his system for free. That's right; the player pays nothing for the system. The scammer meets the sucker in the casino, and if the sucker wins, the scammer takes a percentage of the win—somewhere between 25 and 50 percent. So if the sucker loses, the scammer pays nothing; if the sucker wins, he must share his win with the scammer. Naturally the money risked is that of the sucker. If he loses, he loses his money, not the scammer's money. If he wins, the scammer delightfully pockets some of those wins and heads off into the night (or morning or day).

The really outrageous scammers will even send you their foolproof systems for free by mail, or even by email, and you are on your honor to pay up to 50 percent of your win the first time you use the scammer's advice. The scammer trusts in the honor of enough people to send him checks for his system, an honor the scammer surely lacks. And guess what? Enough people actually send this creep some of their wins!

The next common system is based on a Martingale style of play, an increase in your bets when you lose to make up for previous losses by finally getting a big win that covers all previous losses. In a table game, the usual progression is to double your bet after a loss—$5, $10, $20, and so on. The sucker who plays this method thinks to himself, *Well, I can't lose every bet. I've got to win one of them, right?* Wrong.

On slot machines the Martingale is somewhat different and can be used as a progressive Martingale after losses or also a progressive Martingale after wins. You take a certain amount of money to play the quarter slots, and if you lose all that money (or enough of that money), you go up to $1 slots with a new bankroll. The idea is that since you lost on the quarter slots, your luck will change while you are playing those $1 machines. If you get creamed on the $1 machines, you go up to $5 machines. If you have enough money, you can find yourself playing $25 machines. Imagine the losses you can have doing such a deadly up-as-you-lose system.

The positive-progressive Martingale is usually employed by the scammers who give away their advice for free. The scammer is looking to win a handsome chunk of change from even a few sorry slot players with his ugly system. So what does he want the buyer to do? If you win on the lower-denomination machines after a certain amount has been put through them, then take your new bankroll to a higher denomination and try to double or triple that amount. If you can do that, then send up to 50 percent of your win to the scammer to thank him for his free advice.

You know, I wish I could promise you untold riches on the advantage machines I will recommend that you play. Unfortunately I can't do that. You'll note that the wins are small to moderate with an occasional big one. But even when machines are in a positive mode, you can still lose if the jackpot hit isn't big enough to cover the money you have put into the machine. Yes, you can lose even in advantage play. That's the truth of it in all forms of casino play—be it a negative or a positive expectation for the player. You just don't win all the time.

Scammers are not interested in honesty. They are interested in stupidity—your stupidity for believing them to be truthful about their ridiculous assertions.

So be wary if the offer from a slot seller sounds too good. It is.

CHAPTER 18
Who Plays the Machines?

Everyone. See you next chapter.

Okay, okay, I did this once before as a joke in a magazine article. I just opened and simultaneously ended the article with a single-word answer (I was young, I was foolish, I was fired), but I will actually answer the question I have asked (my editor wants that, too). I do realize that readers want a lot more than generalities when it comes to their favorite games, especially when it comes to other people who play their favorite games. So who plays the slot machines? I'm guessing you do, but there are many others. Let's meet them.

"When table-game players ask me what I play, I am embarrassed when I say I play slots," states Mary J., an Atlantic City slot player and a Wall Street executive. "I tell them I just don't understand the table games, and that's why slots are my thing. The truth is, I really do understand the table games because they aren't that hard to understand. The casinos aren't looking for brain surgeons to play the tables, are they? No. But I like slot machines because they give me the chance to do my own thing without other players around me, and I also don't like table games. But tell that to a table-game player, and they look at you as if you are nuts. So I make it look as if the table-game player is so much smarter than me, but of course he isn't. But it does shut them up. I look at it as different strokes for different folks."

* * *

"I work with the public all day long in my job," says Jim Harris of Nevada, a real-estate broker. "Actually I own the whole company, and I am under a lot of pressure. I can't be yelling and screaming all day when I am having problems with my customers or my staff even when I am wound up, which I often am because mine is a high-stress business. I need to get away from it all, and the slot machines give me that opportunity. I go into my own world; I don't have to deal with other people. I don't have to sell anything or be friendly and nice on a bad day as I must do in my business. It is a relaxing time for me. I call it my private meditation. It releases a lot of stress."

* * *

"Now this may strike you as crazy, but I don't even care what the payback is on the slot machines I play," states Jonathan Davis, a teacher from Illinois. "I pick machines that I didn't play last time, and I stick with one machine the whole time for my play when I am playing. Why do I play the slots? Because I want to think about all the money I can win if I hit it lucky. My teacher's salary isn't all that high. Yeah, yeah, I know the slots have terrible edges for the players, but I can win a lot on the slots, and I just can't do that on the table games playing $5 a hand. The slots I play open the doors to wealth."

* * *

"If you look around, you will see with your own eyes that women play those machines," says Sheri Koehler, a divorce lawyer and an Atlantic City player. "I think the men go for video poker more, and the women play the slots more. Why? I think the women don't want to be hassled by some of the obnoxious table-game players who are always interfering in how you play, telling you what to do, criticizing you, and that kind of thing. Maybe in the years to come you will see even more men play the slots. I remember a time when almost no men played the slots, so the fact that two out of every three casino players play those machines tells you the machines are dominating the casinos more than ever before. But at this moment, yes, the women are the big slot players."

* * *

"I play the slots as a break from table games," says Timothy Barrington, a civil servant from Los Angeles. "I find that if I have had a really bad streak at the tables, I move over to slots, and it calms me down. Sometimes I have been really lucky, hit a big jackpot, and made back all the money I lost at the table games in a few seconds. I don't separate the slot machines from the table games in my mind. It's all gambling, and it's all luck. You get lucky at either type of game, and you win; you get unlucky, and you lose. That's the way it is. You have to accept that fact when you gamble in a casino."

* * *

"I like machines where you get to make choices but not like video poker, which I find really boring, so much that it gives me a headache," states Benjamin Cohen, age 49, an accountant from Illinois. "I'd like to see a machine where you decide certain aspects of what is going to come up. Like if you had a Wheel of Fortune, where you pick which color will come up on the bonus game, and if that one does come up, you get double the prize. That would add a lot of excitement to the games. When you get to make choices, then you are really involved."

* * *

"I like the machines of the past, those three-reelers with no fancy graphics," says Mary L., age 74, a retired bank teller from New York. "You find fewer and fewer of those machines and more of the movie-star ones. I got to tell you I hate the machines with movie-star labels. Who cares about them? You go to the movies to see them; I don't want them on a slot machine. Instead of paying movie stars for their names and images on machines, give us far better paybacks on the machines—all slot players would appreciate that. You can even advertise that this machine is dull and boring but pays back a lot of money, the highest percentage in the whole casino. I think players would rather play that if they knew it was really loose. Screw the movie star and movie and television stuff."

* * *

"Give me a video game where you get to fight someone else who is also playing the machine," says Troy Napolitano, age 27, a teacher from Los Angeles. "The casino can take a cut out of the profits when a player wins a round. That would be edgy and a lot of fun. Most of the slot machines are the same old stuff just repackaged into new-looking models, but they are just as boring as the old models. I want interactive machines where you are at war with one or more players. I really don't care about Elvis Presley or Star Wars."

* * *

"I love the big progressives, but I think they should have one that starts at $50 million and goes up from there," says Donna Slattery, age 37, a business assistant from San Francisco. "The only reason I play machines is to dream about all the money I could get if I win a big jackpot. So give us jackpots that make our mouths water. I really don't care if these machines are tight or loose, I want the thrill of knowing I could buy an island paradise if I won."

* * *

"I hate the machines that pretend to offer you nickel games but really suck you in with so many lines you wind up playing so much money that you can't even keep track of what you are playing," says Carla T., age 66, a retired hairdresser from New Jersey. "I love coming to Vegas, but these new machines are not fun to play because you have no idea of what you are playing and how you are winning or why you are losing. I don't want to sit at a machine and be confused. I want it all spelled out for me. Slot machines should be simple. If we wanted something complicated, we'd play blackjack."

* * *

"Okay, call me old-fashioned or a dope, but I don't like the new paper machines," states Marty Friedman, age 54, a doctor from Texas. "I want to put coins in, and I want to hear real coins coming out when I win. Have you listened to those phony sound recordings of the old-time slots?

Do they sound real? They sound like the fake laughter on those crummy sitcoms that are on television. You could divide the casino up and have half the slots in one part of the casino be real slot machines with real money, and the other half of the casino could be the new paper machines. You know changes in life are not always good, and many of us are sad to see those old machines becoming less and less. They are a remnant of the past, a past I liked."

***

Jerry, a truck driver from Mississippi, said, "I want machines that pay me something once in a while. I have been down almost all the time when I play."

***

Sandra M. Dubowski, retired, has been playing slots in Vegas since the early 1960s and then in Atlantic City since Resorts, the first Atlantic City casino, opened, and she has seen many changes. "All I used to want in the old days when I was young was just to win any kind of money. I'd take any win. Now I dream of hitting it big to send my great-grandchildren to good colleges and not be strapped for money. I've never really come close to that. My biggest win was about $2,400. I spent it in about two weeks and then went back to my losing ways!"

***

Mary Livingston, a housewife from New Jersey, wouldn't give her age. "I'm old enough to know better than to think I will win on the slots in the long run because I *am* in the long run, and boy those slots are rough. My best day I won $12,000 in three different Atlantic City casinos. I kept hitting those intermediate jackpots, and I never was down from the very first spin, which I won. I never had another day like that where I was just so lucky. I've hit some big ones, like on the Blazing Sevens, but I never had a day where I just kept winning. Unfortunately, it wasn't enough to keep me ahead for my slot-playing career. None of my friends are ahead either. I sometimes wonder if anyone is ever ahead for their lifetime of playing the slots."

* * *

"You want advice about slot machines?" laughed Barney Greenburg, a retired accountant from Chicago. "Because I have no advice. I just play them for fun, and I never expect anything. I know I can't beat them, but I have had some really great days. I have won $10,000 a couple of times, and once I had a day where I won about $20,000. That really sounds good, but I've had so many losing trips that even those big wins can't throw me over the top. So my advice is to make sure you aren't playing with money you need for other things and just enjoy yourself. Get out of your head that you are going to make enough to live the life of your dreams. It isn't going to happen."

* * *

"My girlfriend, Rosie, and I used to play as a team," said Olivia LaRusso of New Jersey, a retired schoolteacher. "We would pool an equal amount of money and hit the machines. If we won, we shared the win, and if we lost, we shared the loss. It was very exciting in those days. We had some great wins too. One time both Rosie and I had great days, both of us winning over five figures. We went home and showed our husbands all those $100 bills," She smiled. "My husband said that he loved me even more now that I was rich. He was a funny, lovely guy. Rosie was a great friend too. I miss them both."

Meet the Old Ones

I see them on the Boardwalk, the last stragglers of the greatest generation. Many use walkers now. Many use canes. Some are in wheelchairs. Some hardy few are still robust and chipper, despite being in their eighth or ninth decade. They are the generation that defeated the Nazis and Imperial Japan and fought the communists worldwide since the Korean War and during the Cold War—and won! These are the men and women of the 1930s, the 1940s, the 1950s, and the early 1960s.

No politician such as Lyndon Johnson created the Great Society— no, these great people created it through hard work, family ties, love, and discipline. They are the ones who brought down the Berlin Wall and crushed the Soviet Union while they were at it.

They are our parents and grandparents and great-grandparents now.

When I first started my casino-playing career in the mid-1980s, I would go to Atlantic City a couple of times a week. In those days the midweek Atlantic City crowd was mostly the World War II and Korean War generations. The casinos catered to them because these were the folks who kept the daytime gaming alive and well. Hundreds of buses came and went from Atlantic City every day, and every casino had its own bus trade. It was the Frank Sinatra, Dean Martin, and Sammy Davis Jr. time in the land of the casinos. Wayne Newton was a kid. The Four Seasons hadn't yet hit the winter of their lives.

The weekends in those days of the mid-1980s had a heady mix of these war veterans and their ladies. My mentor, the Captain—the world's greatest craps player—and most of his high-rolling Crew were from the greatest generation of WWII. They dominated the casinos, and therefore most of the entertainment and special events were geared to them.

Today some of the Atlantic City casinos have little or no bus trade—and there are some who don't even want it. The WWII and Korean War old-timers are not as prevalent anymore, nor as welcomed as before, because many of the big-time high rollers from this generation have passed away. The old women significantly outnumber the old men. Small-denomination slot play, with limited bankrolls, prevails. Buffets have replaced gourmet for the remnants of the greatest generation.

So that partly explains why the casinos have installed those penny and nickel machines—that can be played with dozens of coins—to lure small-stakes players into playing more money than they ought to. These particular machines have remarkably high house edges in order to suck the money out of small-stakes players.

While there are still old-timers on the Boardwalk of Atlantic City, their numbers have decreased noticeably. We are losing the greatest generation, and the casinos have started to cater to the younger crowd as mega-casinos such as Borgata steam up the shore and heat up the Strip. The casinos know that in free-spending youth there is money.

Yes, Vegas has drastically changed from its 1990s attempts to paint itself as a "family destination," and it now pushes itself as the sexiest, most scintillating city in the country—which it probably is. The old-timers are not the crowd Vegas is shooting for, although the local casinos still have some of them coming in to play. They want the 40-, 50-, and 60-somethings who have money to blow.

Still, the old-timers are there—if you look for them. Walk up and down the slot aisles in Atlantic City or any casino venue, especially during the day, especially during midweek, and you'll see them. Gray hair, orange hair, blue hair, and no hair, mostly women but some men, playing the slots, talking, relaxing, eating at the buffets, often using their discount coupons. Some writers I've read think these old-timers are a sad sight, as they play games that can't be beaten. Shouldn't these old folks be on some porch somewhere, in some assisted-living or nursing home, out of our sight and not risking their money in the casinos?

Of course, the writers who lament the old-timers spending money on frivolous games probably don't realize that just about everyone who plays casino games must lose in the long run, and most of them also lose in the short run, especially if they are playing low-denomination slot machines where house edges are usually in the double digits.

The old-timers are not playing the machines in order to supplement their incomes. They aren't even necessarily playing the machines to hit the big one. They are playing the machines because they can *still play* the machines! Going to Atlantic City once or twice a month is a great excursion for them. It's a trip where they get to socialize, enjoy the ride, the Boardwalk, the meals, and some slot play.

Most of the WWII generation are in their late 80s now, many over 90. The Korean War generation is starting to scratch those high-water marks too. Their children are grown, and so are many of their grandchildren. Many are great-grandparents—some are even great-great-grandparents.

For life to have full meaning, it must encompass the past, the present, *and* the future. For many old-timers, that last ingredient is often missing from their lives. They talk about the past, and their bodies live in the present, but they have no future to look forward to. The goals of youth are long since gone; the goals of young adulthood have passed; their time, their music, their hold on the world at large is largely gone. They are no longer the movers and shakers of the universe or even the movers and shakers of their own little worlds or even their singular selves.

Going to casinos, strange as this might sound, is a great way to incorporate the future into the present. It's something to look forward to, something to plan for and daydream about. It's something old-timers can do on their own—they set the pace, they determine when and how much to play, and they are in control. When they are in a casino, they are the center of the world—the entire casino's action swirls around them.

I did a little off-the-cuff survey on my last trip to Atlantic City. I sat at slot machines next to the old-timers and struck up conversations. Most of them told me that they budget between $50 to $200 per trip to play the machines but that the real reason they come to the shore is, as one woman put it, "To have an adventure. I don't know if I will win or lose. I don't know the outcome. It's fun to have this suspense. I like the whole atmosphere from the moment I get on the bus. The biggest adventure in my real life is usually going to the doctor. This is a lot more fun."

Indeed, slot machines are fun, and they can be even more fun if you know which ones to play and how to play them.

You've seen those car bumper stickers: *I'm spending my grandchildren's inheritance!* Most people who see that statement smile or laugh. After all, those grey-haired older folks have usually worked very hard for their money and deserve to have some fun with their dough. As they say, "Make bread while the sun shines!"

That bumper sticker works really well on a luxury car too: *See what I'm driving? Take that, son of my son!*

Still, I remember an article in a magazine decrying the fact that so many old people went to Atlantic City during the week on buses and trains and by car to gamble at the slots. The writer of the article said all the people had really sad faces as they were throwing away all their retirement income on the one-armed bandits. These poor (as in pathetic) oldsters were sheep being led to the slaughter, seriously depressed lemmings about to leap from a very high cliff to their economic death. Some he characterized as demented.

To him the men were merely wallets waiting to be waylaid by the casinos; the women were purses the casinos were snatching.

After reading that piece, I took a tour of a weekday Atlantic City in the late spring to see if what I had read was accurate. The old folks were out en masse at this time of the year, and their faces looked nothing like what that writer had portrayed—just the opposite. These folks looked quite happy.

Oh, yes, there were some grumpy-looking faces, but my guess was that these people were grumpy at home, at weddings, at parties too. A grump is a grump no matter where he or she is. You can move the grumpy people physically, but they always bring the grumpiness with them.

I remember when I used to work as a teacher and some seemingly depressed teenager would say, "I won't be as miserable when I'm an adult; everything will be better." I would tell him or her, "You bring yourself with you into adulthood. You don't change unless you change right now. There are no miracles in the future just because it is the future." True. Most of the idiots you knew in high school are probably still idiots today.

So I walked the Boardwalk and closely watched some of these people catching some sunshine while others sat on benches catching up on stories and perhaps the latest gossip with several of their friends. Some fed those obnoxious skydiving, poop-popping seagulls and those over-stuffed pigeons.

Were these old people actually spending their grandchildren's inheritance? The answer was no. Most gave themselves a certain amount to spend, maybe $100 or $200 at most, and they stayed within these limits. They had the magical money-management formula. Use little but maximize fun with it.

Interestingly enough, many of them only played one coin in the machines so as to spread out their playing time for as long as possible or to reduce the overall hit on their bankrolls. They were anything but sheep or lemmings. They were just regular people having some fun.

Then I asked myself the questions, "Why shouldn't the senior-citizen crowd be able to spend their money on entertainment? Why shouldn't they be able to have some fun gambling in the casinos? Did they lose these rights once they hit 75?"

The answers were simple. It's their money; they should be able to spend it as they wish. I'm not talking about those few with a gambling problem—most of these tend to be younger people anyway—but the normal senior citizen who just wants a little juice injected into his or her life.

I am now going out and buying one of those bumper stickers as a symbol of living the life I want to as opposed to the life some depressing writer wants me to lead.

CHAPTER 19

The Ghost in the Machine

"The truth is out there," or so said Fox Mulder of *The X-Files* fame.

When it comes to the truth about slot machines, who knows where the truth lies or what lies are lies, in fact, or what truths are truths or what the heck this sentence means. Many players claim that they have had psychic experiences that led them to win at the slot machines—some of these are pretty big wins, too.

I've received many letters from readers asking me to write more about the psychic dimension of slot machines. I have many of these letters in a file, and I will share some of them with you. Unfortunately I lost a couple hundred letters when my old computer crashed—I couldn't psychically predict that! Here we go:

"I have never had an ESP experience until one day I was playing a slot machine, and I looked up and saw a machine about 20 feet away. I just knew in that instance the machine would hit for me, and I ran over to get to it before anyone else could. I put in about $40, and then all hell broke loose. I won over $20,000! I've never had that feeling happen to me since then. I wish I had!"

***

"These ghosts I see at the slot machines are from the 1950s, and they are all very depressed but well dressed. They are almost all women in evening gowns throwing coins into the machine and pulling the handles. None of the ghosts talk to each other. They seem sleepy and down in the dumps. I don't know if one ghost even knows there are other ghosts around them."

***

"Frank, you are going to think I am nuts, but several times I have sensed machines calling to me. It was as if the machines had some kind of mind or consciousness. I have gone over to these machines and played them with great results. I have won almost every time. The machines don't call to me all the time, but when they do, I now follow that call wherever it may lead, even to very high-priced machines."

***

"You are a math weenie, who believes in math over everything in gambling, aren't you, Scobe? Well math can't explain the psychic dimension of the world we live in. That dimension exists in the world of the slot machines just as it exists in the world at large or in church or wherever else humans gather. I know this for a fact, because I have been able to tap into the psychic world and discover which machines were about to get hot and which machines were about to get cold. I walk through the casinos with my sixth sense at its height to find the machines with my psychic talent. It always works."

***

"The world is full of vibrations, and I can feel those vibrations when I am in Las Vegas, and sometimes all this vibratory energy will lead me to place bets on certain slot machines, and I tend to win on these about 80 percent of the time. I don't know what this is about, but it means something in the larger scheme of things."

***

"I never believed in ESP or any of that crazy stuff until my wife told me she had a dream that a machine somewhere on the casino floor would hit. She could see the machine in the dream, and we both got dressed quickly and headed right to the casino to see if we could find this machine. I was humoring her. We walked around, and then she stopped me and said she saw the machine. An old lady was sitting there playing it. Sure enough the machine hit big time. We weren't on it, but my wife knew that was the machine she had dreamt about."

* * *

"How do you explain that my mother-in-law almost never loses on the slots? She says she just knows what machines will hit, and those are the machines she plays. My mother-in-law is an honest woman, and I don't think she is lying to me."

* * *

"Scobe, I just touch the machines, and the ones that are going to pay out have a different vibration than the ones that are not going to pay out. This good vibration is like electricity, but the bad vibration is like an upset stomach."

* * *

"There are ghosts in the slot areas of almost every casino from people who loved playing the machines and couldn't give them up until they were a part of big wins. They died but still wanted the action of the machines. These ghosts just feel like they have unfinished business and must wander around the slot floors of the casinos. But being supernatural creatures, they tend to gather around machines that are about to hit. . They derive energy from these machines. Being a psychic, I can see these ghosts with my inner eyes, and when they are gathered at a machine, I get on it if it is empty and go for the big win. I've gotten that win a lot."

* * *

"I find the hot machines by gauging the temperature of the area near the machine and around the machine. The nature of the atmosphere reflects the nature of what is going on at the center of the activity. Why are warm days the best days for fires? A hot machine will heat up the world around it. If you are sensitive enough, you can feel that little extra heat. That is the machine you should play."

***

"Mr. Scobe, I believe that women have more psychic abilities than we men. I always look to see where the most women are playing in the casino because I think their psychic powers have led them to those areas. I think they can presee what is about to happen, maybe in a hazy way, and that's where I go to play. It has been a very good thing too, because I have had many winning sessions in these areas where women congregate."

Okay, the above are from the believers in a magic, mystical notion of playing the machines. But there are just as many people who received psychic vibrations and lost their money too. These psychics saw their perfect machines and got creamed. Their stories are just pathetic and sad and can be summed up as follows: "I got this vibration that I would win on this machine, and I lost every penny that I had."

But why bother with the sad stories? It would be fun if psychic experiences could really help us win at the slots or win at anything in life.

CHAPTER 20

Slot Advertising

In all gambling magazines and newspapers are pictures of wondrously happy winning slot players holding monstrously large checks with big monetary figures on them. You'll probably see tens of thousands, hundreds of thousands, and maybe even millions of dollars on these huge checks. Sometimes there will be a happy casino executive or two with wide smiles on their faces helping to hold these outsized checks for the camera. Many of these outsized pictures will be hung on walls throughout the casino to encourage everyone to think big. And bet big too.

Of course, these cheerful pictures of these happy people and happy casino executives are furnished by the casinos' public-relations departments, and the casinos are swift in getting them out to countless newspapers and magazines. Why not? No casino advertising works as well as showing smiling winners holding their slot dreams in their hands. It's a beautiful sight. Those people are you and me, aren't they? No pretty handsome models for these pictures; they are a slice of humanity, as real as real can be.

Slot players want to see that it is possible to have their fanciful dreams fulfilled, and these pictures do just that. They say to you, "You don't think you can win? Just take a look at Mr. Davis here or Mrs. Davenport there, and see them smiling because they did win! They won a ton of money! That ton of money is out there waiting for you too! It's all sitting in our beautiful slot machines. Go get 'em, kids!"

Nowhere in the accompanying words do the casino public-relations writers mention that these few individuals had to overcome an immense magnitude of odds to get those big checks or that almost all of them are heavily down in their slot-playing career. Why spoil the dream? That would be like saying those few people in the television commercials who went on this certain "no-fail fat-loss diet" and lost upward of 100 pounds actually are not like the 95 percent of the people out there who went on the same damn diet and a year later gained all their weight back...and then some.

Such practical thinking ruins everything. You can't have digital dreams in an analog television set if you do that. "Don't confuse slot players with the awful facts" is the motto of the casinos, and that is understandable. If slot players woke up to what they were actually facing, many wouldn't play most of the machines on the casinos' floors, and where would that leave the casinos?

Slot advertising has to play up two things—the hope that you can win (and maybe win *big*) and the fact that even if you lose your money, as you probably will, the mere playing of those machines is a sheer joy. It's fun whether you win or lose. Ads for slot play never show some forlorn guy sitting at a machine, a beer in his hand, a half-smoked cigarette dangling from his lips, ashes having fallen all over his shirt, with this miserable look on his flaccid, puffy face. They don't show a crazed lady foaming at the mouth kicking a machine after losing 30 spins in a row. What kinds of images would those be for readers to see?

Hey, car commercials want to sell sex, right? (Or is that sex commercials want to sell cars?) Buy this car, and the most beautiful, sexy women on earth will be falling all over you. These commercials don't show a herd of wild, ugly, monstrous female wildebeests snarling and tearing the guy's clothes off because he started driving this great new car. No man would buy the car if that were the result of such a purchase—female werewolves attacking him under the full moon. He has enough problems in his life already.

I remember once at Tropicana in Atlantic City I was in the bathroom, standing at the urinal doing what a man must do, and right in front of me was a picture of a happy slot winner holding one of these outlandish checks. I looked above all the other porcelain urinals and, sure enough, each one had the picture of some happy check-holding winner.

When you are doing what I was doing, you have only two directions in which to look—especially if there are other men doing you-know-what next to you. You look down or up; you never look to the side. If you look up, the casino gives you a message: "When you finish what you are doing, big guy, play some slots, and you might be in the picture holding a big check next time." If you look down...well it isn't a very interesting or rewarding sight, is it? You've seen that sight a million times already. It's no big thing, so to speak.

Of course, the professionally designed magazine ads showing happy slot players smiling happily as they are happily playing those gleaming machines aren't much different than the giant-check pictures, except the professionally designed slot advertisement's colors are far more vibrant, and the deliriously cheering people in the ads are no doubt from some casting agency, not a wildebeest in the lot. Certainly these happy, extremely good-looking people aren't regular folks selected randomly from the slot aisles. Who wants to see a blue-haired bloated grandma in some pumped-up ad about the joys of slot playing? If she wins a big one in the casino, well, the public-relations people will have to stick her in the giant-check picture, but in paid advertising, as we say in Brooklyn, fuggetaboudit! Grandpa of the big belly and the age-spotted skin isn't going to make the advertising cut either. There's no sexiness in post-60-somethings, is there?

Advertising sells dreams. It can't sell reality, because we all have enough reality as it is in our lives. Also, reality is free; we're inundated with reality. Slot advertising isn't going to warn those big winners that every greedy relative and friend will be hitting them up for "loans" that will never be paid back. What fun is that?

Some television slot advertising is also similar to those psychic slot dreams too. One such commercial had a woman walking the casino floor and getting vibrations from the machines. One such machine gave off the best vibration, and she started to play it. The music in the commercial led you to believe she was about to make a killing. The casino where she was playing was then boldly written on the screen. You play in that casino, and these vibrations could lead you to kick this casino's rectum, and then *your* picture can be put above a urinal.

There were some commercials running in a Southern venue where several casinos all claimed to be the "luckiest" casino in that area. Yes, they were *all* the luckiest! How that was possible is hard to fathom, unless there was some kind of quantum mechanics involved in the analysis of their machines. "All these different payback percentages are actually the exact same, even though they are all totally different!" Yes, mind-boggling for sure.

The true irony here is that it is fun to have these giant-check dreams, these vibration-feeling moments, the sense of luck around the corner, as long as the dreams and vibrations don't get out of hand. What's so wrong about looking at the folks in the giant-check pictures and letting your mind fantasize a little? Just don't take an equity loan against your house to play the machines because of such fantasizing.

CHAPTER 21

Slots and Sex

C an you imagine in the late 1940s and in the 1950s—those wonderful decades where television first came into being and quickly grew (like the Blob) to become the rage in American households— watching commercials about (for lack of a better word) *penile* power or, rather, lack of penile power? Those were the days when television's husbands and wives slept in separate beds. Did Donna Reed actually have raunchy dirty sex with her husband, Dr. Alex Stone, to produce her really nice kids? Not possible.

But now on television, the flaccid penis now miraculously made strong as steel by a magic pill that might maybe give a man an erection for four whole hours (if so, he has to go to the hospital—perhaps to astound the doctors and nurses) has become material for commercials. How did that ever happen?

It's a wonder we even created a generation of humans in the 1950s and early 1960s since no one ever seemed to have sex or even talk about sex on television—and television was a reflection of real life, wasn't it? Although my parents and all the parents of all the kids I knew while I was growing up in Bay Ridge, Brooklyn, slept together, I thought that maybe sleeping apart was a suburban thing. That's probably why cities were teeming with people while the suburbs didn't have too many of them in those days.

Oh, yes, in those wonderfully innocent days of early television, there were even advertisements about the benefits of smoking. Smoking was good. Doctors happily proclaimed which cigarette brands they smoked, and cigarette companies proclaimed their surveys proved that their individual cigarettes were the best. Cool and mild, good tasting, just the kind of thing to do in your separate twin bed. I guess husbands and wives had to do something in their individual beds, so why not puff on a cigarette?

Good-looking women smoked; rugged, handsome men smoked. Even a big sign near Times Square smoked! Vegas had cowboy signs that smoked. Everyone in the movies smoked, and everyone in movie theaters did too. I guess everyone had to smoke because they couldn't possibly have sex in those twin beds you saw on the *Adventures of Ozzie and Harriet* show, could they? *Leave it to Beaver* had no double meaning in those days either.

Today it is entirely different. There are dozens of commercials about the joys of having an erection for men who might have been having trouble, you know, down there, because of diabetes, high blood pressure, being overweight, or just advancing age. In these commercials you see happy men and *extremely* happy women walking the beach, arm in arm, loving the joys of life after, you know, doing *that*. And, yes, as stated, some of the commercials even warn you that you shouldn't have an erection for more than four hours! That could be dangerous. Yeah, I would imagine it could be—to the man himself and to any woman within, ah, arm's length of him.

Happily, no one smokes anymore—not before, not during, and not after sex. Near Times Square there is a giant advertisement, not of smoking, but of a woman in her (oh, my, my) *underwear!*

So today everything is about sex, sex, sex, and more sex. Doctors talk about sex on television. Old people talk about sex on television. Even unimaginably ugly people who shouldn't even be allowed to have sex or produce offspring can talk about sex on television. There are even pornographic channels on cable television, which my wife won't let me watch. ("It's research, dear," I said. She said, "You'll be researching a lump on your head from a frying pan too.") The Internet is loaded with sex—if you have children they will see more sex on television and on the Internet than they will ever see cigarette smoking on these mediums.

However, no one has talked about the fact that sex and slot machines are intimately related. And they are. *Intimately.*

Even if you are a senior citizen, you can't be having sex, sex, and more sex all the time—you do need some time to take your various daily medications and a shower, don't you? But there are other reasons for reducing the amount of rumpy-pumpy too.

First, your heart might explode, and that could get messy for your partner since you aren't sleeping in those twin beds anymore, or you might die from so much exertion too. And second, you have to do other things to have a well-rounded life—like, maybe, take a cold shower?

But slot machines are more like the actual act of sex itself—and not just a diversion from sex. That's correct. Slots are like sex in many ways.

Okay, here are some of the similarities between slots and sex. After the first time you had sex, what happened a few hours later? That's right, you wanted more sex. After that? You still wanted more sex. From the first stirrings of puberty until the latest Viagra commercial that just exploded on your television screen waking you from your nap on the couch with the remote firmly clutched in your hands, you have been thinking about sex. It is said that a man thinks about sex every six to eight seconds. I am guessing it is probably more often than that—we might even be in the nanoseconds. And now with all the medical aids available, you can think and have sex until you die, which could be the same exact moment for some people.

And slot players are just like that. You've seen it. Slot players will play some credits, and what happens? Even if they win in a grand explosion of cash, what do they do? They want to play more credits! And then even *more* credits. They can never get enough! And like the sexually voracious society we live in, they are not content to just play one machine. Noooo! They cheat on that machine with other machines! Some slot players are so promiscuous that they go from machine to machine, playing this one and that one, never satisfied with the last machine and always looking for something better. Slot players are the Tiger Woods of casino gamblers.

Some of these slot players are so mechanimalistic that they play two machines at once! Some play three machines! Some of the overheated engorged rich people play whole *banks* of machines!

Slot players are like men overdosing on sexual-enhancement products. It has clearly gotten out of hand (so to speak) with some of them. They need to rest, relax, and maybe have a smoke or another cold shower.

Slot Sex Sirens

I have to warn you that what's coming up now is still more sex—and, no, not the loving kind that exists between spouses or the fiercely romantic kind that exists in great poetry through the ages, but the dirty, sordid, often disgusting kind that is constantly shown on television shows geared toward preteens. Yes, sex of the kind some men will pay for and some women will sell, which is also known as the dangerous kind because you really don't know what you will be getting during or after such sexual encounters.

"What happens in Vegas stays in Vegas"—oh, really? Not true if it concerns germs and viruses. These little devils can hop the plane with you and fly back to your home in Flaccid Falls, Florida.

Now you may wonder how slot machines can actually be about dirty, filthy, often paid-for sex—what do these two things have in common in the real world as opposed to the reel world? Stick with me, and you will find out.

But first a detour of sorts: I have a love of history, and I have been reading about countercultural movements in our civilization—from the Roaring '20s to the beatniks of the 1950s to the artist colonies that have been in America since before the Civil War to the hippies, and I discovered that these movements all had one thing in common. Brush off the black beatnik eyeliner and close your ears to their awful poetry, look past the great music and fabulous dancing of the Roaring '20s, turn off your CD of *Hair*, and what do you find? From way back when through Andy Warhol through Madonna and right up to today's indifferent couplings on the university campuses across America—here is what you find: sex.

It's all about sex. The poetry, the paintings, the music, the dance, the avant-garde, the rap and hip-hop, and all of this and all of that, all of it was a cover-up for mating. Nothing more and nothing less. Mating. Period.

The young discover sex in every generation and think it is some big deal—as if no generation before them discovered it as well. But since they give new names to their discovery of biology ("I'm not in a mating ritual, I am a Goth.") they think what they are doing is brand new because it has a brand-new name.

And that brings me to slot machines. The slot and video-poker machines of the $5 denomination and up variety or those multiline machines that can take oodles of money for all their plays or those 10-game-play or 50-game-play or 100-game-play video-poker and slot machines—and also the bar-top machines—are the point of contact between the women of the night (early mornings and days) and the male slot players. My theory, based on firsthand knowledge from many men and from my own experiences, is that prostitutes work the machines more than they work the table games because at the table games most men don't want to be approached—they are into the game—whereas at a slot machine the man controls the game, and if a "lovely" wiggles up to him to talk, he'll stop playing or talk to her while he is playing. It's also a private encounter not witnessed by everyone else as it would be at the table game.

I have only been approached at a table game a half dozen times in over two decades, but when I am playing a high-denomination machine, I have been approached many times—often many times during the same night!

Many men have had the same experiences as me. It usually goes like this:

"Are you having any luck?" she asks.

"So, so," he says.

"Is your wife here playing the machines?" she says as she looks at the man's wedding ring.

"My wife is not with me on this trip," says the man.

Pause. Sometimes she sprays perfume on herself. Then—

"Why don't we go back to your room and have some fun?" she says.

Now when some variation of this happens to me, I politely inform the young woman that I am not interested. She usually smiles and heads to the next perceived payday. Obviously middle-aged men playing high-denomination machines are good prospects for those women who prowl the night (and the mornings and the days) in Las Vegas and elsewhere. Middle-aged men aren't the only ones, of course, since those young men, giddy on drink and gambling and thinking that deadly sexually transmitted viruses also obey the commercial rule that "what happens in Vegas stays in Vegas" (or Atlantic City or Reno or Lake Tahoe or the Midwest) are fair game as well.

The machines allow a working woman natural cover—two people talking at a machine for a little while does not look like anything sordid or special. Being approached at a table game, which happens infrequently, is noticeable and disruptive.

Probably the best area for the proactive femme fatales continues to be the bars of the various casinos. Here men can drink aplenty and play those bartop machines, and the women can sidle right up to them, ask for a drink, talk to them, and then make their pitch.

It's all about sex.

Okay, I must admit that I am a fuddy-duddy. I think paying for a prostitute is a stupid thing to do. Think logically now: you are going to enjoy an intimate relationship with someone who has slept with the equivalent of every male in Bensonhurst. What are the odds of her having something she caught from one or hundreds of them? I'd say it's the best bet in the house. After all, have you seen the men out there who go to prostitutes?

There's a good chance your working lady is also taking nonprescribed drugs—a practice that is a great way to contract and transmit diseases by the hypodermic full. Putting aside the fact that she might also want to drug you and rob you, the fact is that if you are married, you are cheating on your wife, and if you are not married you are probably cheating on your girlfriend or fiancée.

It really isn't worth the bother. Enjoy gambling with your money when you are in Vegas or elsewhere. Don't gamble with your health. End of sermon.

CHAPTER 22

My Top 10 Weird and Wacky Slot Experiences

10. The Heavyweight Puncher

At Atlantic City's defunct Sands was a man who was fat, bald like Friar Tuck of Robin Hood fame, with a remarkably hairy chest that was totally viewable because he had four buttons undone so he could show off his mohair. Several gold chains entwined in his massive amount of chest hair. He was a ruddy rug of a man.

He lost spin after spin, and then he bellowed like a fat boar, hauled off and punched the machine with all his might, screaming all manner of obscenities at it. What outraged him more than losing was the pleasant woman on the machine two over from his who was winning on almost every other spin and clapping her hands, saying, "This is the luckiest day of my life! Oh, my, the luckiest day of my life!" He almost growled when she would shout that out at the top of her lungs. She must have been an opera singer in her long-passed youth, she was that loud. Everyone heard her and especially him, since he was closer to her than anyone else.

The man's knuckles made a loud sound when they connected with the machine, *Ba-Boom!* Of course, the machine sat passively, showing no evidence of the mighty blow leveled at it. The man didn't stop playing either. On the next spin after slugging the machine, he lost again, just as the woman screamed happily, "I won the jackpot! I won the big jackpot!"

Violence just doesn't pay. You can ask his swollen, bloody hand if it did for him.

9. The Winning Switch

This leather-skinned, unemployed, tanned man never played the slots in his life, but one of his unemployed beach-bum buddies was a guy who was a former slot technician and now told everyone in his circle that he was the world's greatest slot expert. It was this beach bum's claim to fame in his group of welfare recipients. "I am a great slot expert!" he exclaimed to the other unemployed sun worshippers all around him. So the leather-skinned, tanned man told me what the slot technician had told him, "There is a button in the back of all slots that you flip, and then the player wins the money and not the casino. Try it next time, and see if it is true. If the casino wants you to win a few dollars, they will press the button for you. Just press that button in back, and you will win." Next time I was in the casino, I reached around to the back of a machine. The button wasn't there.

8. Painful Win

The Golden Nugget in Las Vegas. I had just finished eating in their fine now-defunct Italian restaurant Stephanos. Okay, yes, I was somewhat happy from a bottle of fine wine as I was heading to the bathroom. I passed a machine, I think it was called Treasure Island, put in three coins, and hit for $1,600. I then had to wait to be paid. And wait. And wait. It was the most *excruciatingly painful* win I ever had in my life. You might say that win was almost a real pisser.

7. Red Hair versus Blue Hair

At the Showboat in Atlantic City in the 1990s, two elderly women were playing the slots side by side until the blue-haired one had to go to what she called "the powder room." The red-orangey-haired one then took over the blue-haired one's machine because the blue-haired one had been winning and the red-orangey-haired one had been losing. When blue-hair came back she told the red-orangey-haired one to "get off my machine!" The red-orangey-haired grandmotherly looking woman delicately answered, "Go to hell, you bitch!" Then they fought. They punched weakly at each other and pulled out some of each other's strangely colored hair. I grabbed the blue-haired one, another man grabbed the red-orangey-haired one, and the fight stopped. Oh, by the way, these two women were sisters.

6. Caveman

This happened at a now-defunct downtown Vegas casino. This casino was packed because of a big promotion. An attractive older woman sitting next to a big guy said to me, "Excuse me, sir, but could you tell this man he smells?" The man, hearing her, turned to the woman and said, "Why don't you tell me yourself, you old bag?" I stepped up to the man and smiled, "Oh, sir," I started, and then I caught a whiff of him. Something, probably many things, had died on this guy's body. "Oh God," I groaned. Now what would you do in a situation like this? I turned to the woman and said in a whisper, "Go play another machine. You could die here." And she said, "This is my favorite machine. Tell him to leave." "I ain't leaving," said Stinko. There was only one thing I could do for this old woman who was in distress—I left.

5. Pretty Pregnant

She was pretty and pregnant. She was very pregnant and playing the Blazing 7s at Tropicana. The pregnant woman called over to me. I thought she said, "My glass of water broke." I walked over. "Where's the glass? I don't want anyone to step on the glass," I said. "Glass? My water broke! I'm about to have a baby!" Being cool, I responded, "Uh, ah, ee, oh, aaaarrrggghhhh!" and luckily one of the female security guards took it from there. This lady hit the jackpot that day, even though she lost her money on the machines.

4. Wasted Luck

A big-name casino in Las Vegas. The kid was young, maybe 16, but he had snuck in and was playing a machine when he hit a big one just as the security guard came over to ask for his identification. Ooops! Sorry, kid, you lose. The kid argued, so did the kid's parents, so did the kid's lawyer.

The casino won. The kid lost. If good luck is a finite commodity, this kid probably used up most of his.

3. Gloating

I entered the elevator of this premium Vegas hotel. A couple entered—the wife laughing, the husband singing. "We won a ton of money tonight," laughed the wife. "Oh, yeah! Oh, yeah! Oh, yeah!" sang the husband. "How did *you* do?" the wife asked me. "I got killed," I said. "Well, too bad," she laughed. "Oh, no! Oh, no! Oh, no for you chum!" sang the husband. Chum? *Chum?* He actually called me "chum." I put up with all of that all the way up to the top floor of penthouse suites. They were so happy for themselves. They danced out of the elevator. I was hoping they would trip on the rug and fall to the floor, getting rug burns. They didn't. Couldn't they have shown a little pity for me? Never gloat at another's misfortune because that could be your misfortune in the future.

2. A Bigger Bucket

In the days of pervasive coin slots, a woman was playing at Bally's. I asked her how she was doing, and she said, "I am almost there." I had no idea what she meant, so she told me. "Oh, when I was younger I wanted a husband, and I found him. I wanted a house, and I got it. I wanted children. They are now all grown up." She looked at me and smiled, "Today I just want to fill a larger bucket than this one. I am almost at the top. That is my goal, to fill up a larger bucket." Actually this isn't a weird story, merely the story of a life well lived.

1. The Magic 7 Slot Magnet

Ages ago, I received a mailing about a "Magic 7 Slot Magnet" that made machines hit like crazy. Being interested in finding out what this great new invention was (the seller claimed that he won millions with it and was now retiring from the casinos to live on his own private island, which I later found out was Alcatraz), I sent in my $39.99.

My Magic 7 Slot Magnet arrived with an added bonus—a Slot Divining Rod that would lead me to hot machines that my Magic 7 Slot Magnet would help me conquer for untold wealth and my own island! (I was thinking Manhattan. I think big.)

At the casino I walked around with this cheap cardboard divining rod trying to locate "loose" machines. People looked at me as if I were crazy. *Screw them,* I thought, *I won't let any of them into Manhattan after I own it.*

Finally, the rod picked out its first machine by bending. I took out my Magic 7 Slot Magnet and moved it over the machine as the directions indicated. The "magnet" was not a real magnet, just a flimsy piece of metal with a poorly embossed slot machine on it. I played a few hundred dollars in the machine. I lost.

For an entire evening and much of the next day, I used my divining rod and my Magic 7 Slot Magnet throughout Atlantic City. I won a few spins here and there but overall nothing of note. Even young and dumb, I realized there was no proof in the hype about the Magic 7 Slot Magnet or any power in the flimsy Slot Divining Rod. I went over to Pier One across from Caesars and threw them into the Atlantic Ocean. The divining rod floated out to sea, and the Magic 7 Slot Magnet sunk to the bottom.

And I still don't own Manhattan.

CHAPTER 23

Just Shoot Me!

As a gambling writer I have to spend enough time in all the sections of the casino to get the hang of what's being done, what's being said, and who is whom, what is what, where is where, and all the rest of it. That obviously includes the slot aisles, the big cities of the casino state, where I roam and sit, sit and roam, where I talk to the players and try to unearth the reasons why people play the machines and what brings them back time after time, over and over again, win, lose, or lose some more.

There is not one single slot player I have met who doesn't know that the slots are unbeatable, except with a large sledge hammer and a dream. Oh, yes, there are some advantage-play slot machines that I'll show you in the next chapter, but these are the small exceptions to the slot rule—it ain't easy to win; it ain't easy at all.

So I was sitting at a machine the other night, just getting my bearings, watching the slot players play fast, faster, and so fast that you could hardly count the nanoseconds between spins. Some of these slot players were delirious, as they were winning; more were stone-faced, as they were losing.

And then this woman sat next to me. She was around 70 years old, with a poor facelift that made her mouth look like the cavernous mouth of the horrifying face plastered on the entrance at the old Steeplechase in Coney Island. An Alfred E. Newman kind of face pulled tight as if it were a rubber rope in a tug-of-war contest. You could see the stretch marks that lined her jaw as the skin was pulled behind her ears. Her face couldn't move much, except that her voice box still worked. I think she had been overdosed on botox too, since her forehead looked like a Klingon's.

"I just love playing the slots," she said through all that stretched skin.

"Ah, good, good, have fun," I said.

"Are you playing? I haven't seen you spin the reels."

"Oh," I said. "I was just thinking here a bit."

"What were you thinking about?"

"Nothing, really, just wandering thoughts," I said.

"Now how can a person think of nothing? Isn't that a contradiction in terms?"

"I didn't mean exactly nothing," I said. "You know, just kind of like thoughts going by and other thoughts following them. That's what I mean by nothing."

"People should say what they mean and not say what they don't mean," she stated authoritatively.

"I guess you're right," I said.

"Of course I am right," she said. "Listen, if you aren't playing that machine, can you exchange seats with me? Your machine is going to get lucky, and I want to be playing it when it does. I can sense hot machines."

"Oh, yes, fine," I said and got up. This was my chance to get away, and I made a step to head down the aisle, but she caught me with her voice.

"Now you sit right down next to me, young man. I have some things I want to talk to you about."

"I don't have much time," I said, looking at my wrist, where I forgot to put my watch on.

"This will only take a minute," she said. So I sat down, which was a mistake.

"I come to Vegas alone, you know," she said. "My husband ran off with another woman who was 30 years his junior, and he hasn't spoken to me since our divorce. That was 20 years ago. I hear he's still married to that thing. Men are animals, if you ask me. That woman never even talked when I met her. She worked with him, and I rarely heard her speak."

"Sorry about that," I said.

"About men being animals? About her not speaking?"

"No, no, about your former husband," I said.

"Why should you be sorry? You didn't do anything."

"Right, you know, that's just a phrase," I said. "Just to let you know I sympathize with you."

"An incorrect phrase," she said. "Our language has many incorrect phrases."

"Yeah, yeah, you're right."

"Of course," she nodded. "I studied logic in college, and that is why I am so logical." She put a $100 bill into the machine. "My husband was an illogical man. He couldn't stand for me to tell him why his thinking processes were wrong. Ooohhh, I almost had a big one on that spin. Look how close the symbols came to being in line."

"Actually, they just look like they are close, but being above the correct line is as far away as if you never saw those symbols," I said.

"Is that nonsense or what? There are the symbols, just one line away. You are saying that they are not one line away? How illogical can you get? Can't you see they are one line away?"

Do I argue with her or shut up? Over my years of writing about the games we all play, I have found it a wise practice to just keep my mouth shut in the casinos when it comes to advice or knowledge or both. Most casino players don't want advice, and they don't want knowledge; they just want to have whatever their definition of fun is. So I kept my mouth shut.

"You have no answer for me, I see," she laughed. "Never argue with a woman of logic." Her face didn't move when she laughed. It was as if she had a soundtrack in her neck that just erupted from her marbled face. If I had been her husband, I would have run away too—preferably with a mute, as he evidently did.

"Okay, well, I gotta go," I said.

"I have a question for you," she said as if I had never said a thing about leaving. I paused. "You see that woman over there? The one with the premature wrinkles?"

"Yes," I said, looking over.

"Would you want to take her out to dinner tonight, my treat? I'll pay for everything."

"What?"

"That's my daughter," she said, "and she's a very depressed person because she hasn't landed a man yet. All the men she's dated, they leave her flat after a while. She's 48 years old, and she is miserable. If you—"

"No, no," I said. "I'm married. I'm happily married. I am sure your daughter is very nice…"

"Ha! She's an idiot!" the lady said. "She even had a shot twice at two very rich men, and she blew the whole thing with both of them. These guys weren't anything to look at, they were fat pigs, but she could have fooled around after she got hitched, you know?"

"Well, I gotta go," I said.

"Your wife doesn't have to know…"

"Look, I am sure that you have your reasons for this, but I am just not interested," I said.

"Nonsense," she said. "You're in Vegas, where it is expected you fool around."

"No, no," I said. "No, not for me. I told you I love my wife."

"Terry, come over here!" she shouted. Terry looked up and shambled over. My word, this woman really did look depressed.

"This young man wants to take you to dinner," said the woman.

Terry looked me up and down. She had blue-black bags under dull gray eyes. She sniffed. Her nose was running, and she dabbed a handkerchief at it. Okay, so I no longer looked like Cary Grant or Brad Pitt, but I wasn't the Elephant Man either. Terry kept staring at me and then shook her head no and turned away from me.

"Listen, young lady," scolded the woman. "You can't be too choosy, you know. This nice young man…."

"I'm over 60 years old," I said.

"You look older," said Terry. "You have too much weight on you. I don't like fat people. No offense." She rubbed the handkerchief against her dripping nose.

"She had a nose job about 10 years ago that didn't take properly. That's why her nose runs," said the woman. "No big deal. Just don't look at it dripping all the time."

"No offense taken, Terry. You see, I am married," I said.

"And you are looking to cheat on your wife?" said Terry disdainfully as she daubed her running nose.

"No, no," I said.

"You don't want to go to dinner with this man? What is your name?" she asked me.

"Fr...Fra...Fritz," I stammered.

"Fritz what?" asked Terry.

"Lang," I blurted. *Please God, don't let her know who Fritz Lang was. Why did I say Fritz Lang?*

"Look," I said.

"Mother, this gentleman is looking for a one-night stand cheating on his wife. I do not do those anymore." Anymore? Anymore? I looked her over. She wasn't exactly devastatingly beautiful. I mean she wasn't a howling mangy mongrel, but she was coming pretty close with that wet nose.

"Listen, I think you got this all wrong," I said.

"What would your wife think of this, Fritz?" asked Terry.

"Fritz? Who? What? Oh, oh, you mean Fritz, you mean me; that's me; no, look I do not want to have dinner, and I am not looking for a one-night stand!" Unfortunately, I said that too loud. Several women in the slot aisle turned and looked at me reproachfully.

"You would do that to your wife?" shouted a somewhat soused lady at the end of the bank of machines.

"I am not doing anything to my wife!" I said to her.

"Well, you should, that's your duty as a husband, don't you know?" shouted the soused one.

"If you took care of your wife you'd not be looking for a hookup," reproached Terry.

"I'm not looking for a hookup!"

Now many heads in the slot aisle turned my way. I guess this was an added entertainment feature for them.

"I am gonna get hot now!" shouted the stretched-faced mother of the wet-nosed daughter. "Those big symbols appeared again right above the line."

Three women and two men continued to frown at me from their machines. Terry was sniffing and dabbing her dripping nose. Terry's logical mother with her wretchedly stretched face and Klingon forehead started to hammer away at the slot machine, lost in her nutty world of a "lucky" machine.

"Excuse me," I said loudly. "I have to go meet my harem."

"Men like you disgust me," said Terry, licking some drip off her upper lip.

I hustled from the slot aisle and headed for the elevators to tell my wife, the beautiful AP, what just happened.

You certainly meet all types in a casino.

CHAPTER 24
Advantage Slot Machines

Author's note: *The great advantage player Jerry "Stickman" has collaborated with me on the next two chapters. Without him, these chapters would not exist. We all owe this man a big thank you!*

This chapter will show you specific machines that can actually give the player an edge over the casinos at slots. These machines have been discovered by Jerry "Stickman" and have been put through extensive computer studies and casino play.

That's right. Smart slot players can now get a real edge over the house if they play these machines properly. Jerry "Stickman" discovered which machines to play and how and when to play them. He analyzed what minimum bankrolls are needed for each machine and also which machines are volatile—that is, which machines will give you wild swings of wins and losses.

These machines can be considered "banking machines" because they build up redeemable credits, objects, or multipliers that are not wiped out when one player leaves the machine and another player replaces him. In fact, you will need these other players to play these machines in a negative mode so that the banking credits build up for you.

However, at a certain point the "accumulated bank" causes the machine to become positive for any player who plays the machine from that point onward. In short, more money will come out of the machine from that point than goes in the machine. That is when you play the machine. And guess what? The machine will tell you when it is in positive mode based on how much has been banked. The banking will be in various saved symbols on the machines, as you will see.

There's money to be made by playing these machines in positive modes.

Let's get the obvious question out of the way for the dreamers in the land of slots. Yes, while *some* of your wins can be fairly big, *most* of them will not be fairly big but somewhere in the land of reasonable. But all will make you smile because you are doing something very few players have ever done: getting an edge over the casino at the slot machines. Yes, you can also lose, because even in a positive mode machines can take your money. In poker that's called a bad beat. You have a great hand and still lose. But overall, play these machines just the way you are told to play them, and the money will be coming out to you much more than the money going in for the casino.

Playing advantage slot machines has little or no risk for the player of being barred from play in the casino as playing advantage blackjack, craps, or Pai Gow could, and it is totally nonstressful. It requires no skill. If you can feed money into the machine and push a button, you can play the game. Wouldn't it be great to add a game such as this to your advantage-play toolkit—one that can be played when you aren't able to play other advantage-play games? You can also play these machines to relax between your play at the tables. Putting your slot card in will also add to your pleasure, since you'll be playing with an advantage at the machine and the casino might also be giving you comps. Ah, the joy of it all!

A Different Type of Slot Machine

This type of advantage slot machine is similar to progressive slot machines in the sense that something builds. It is not a jackpot dollar amount though. Instead *something else* builds. It could be coins, hats, gems, fruit, or even firecrackers. It can be almost anything.

The pool of items builds when a special symbol or some combination of symbols appears on the reels. This can be one particular symbol, a combination of symbols, or even the absence of symbols sometimes called blanks or ghosts. For example, if a cherry appears in one of the nine positions that are visible on the reels, a cherry is added to the corresponding section of a pie. Each different machine has its own criteria for saving.

Once a certain combination of symbols appears or a section of the collection area is filled, a bonus is paid that is proportionate to the number of hats, gems, fruit, or whatever symbol that's been banked. For example, a diamond is added to one of three columns corresponding to the reel that contains a diamond. When a column is filled with diamonds, a bonus of 10 credits is collected, and the column is emptied.

The more things that are in the collection, the better chance the game might be positive. And this chapter will show you *which* games can become positive as well as *when* they become positive. It will give you the best method to play them and let you know how much money you should have available once you decide to play a given advantage machine. A proper bankroll is absolutely necessary to give yourself the best chance to win.

General Rules for Playing Advantage Slots

Once you have found a game that has a positive expectation, there are certain rules you must follow to maximize your wins. Some may seem obvious, but it is amazing how quickly one can forget about discipline when one is playing and winning. The following rules for play are not suggestions—they are *requirements*. They must be followed if you are going to maintain an advantage.

Here goes:

1. **Only play when you have an advantage.** This rule applies while playing any casino game. You must recognize that playing without an advantage negates any wins you might have in the short run. If the house has the edge, then you will ultimately lose your money. It is hard work to win money from a casino. Don't give it back. Only play when you have an advantage.

2. **Have the required bankroll in your pocket.** Once you have determined that you have an advantage at a machine, you must play until you collect the bonus or jackpot. Lady Luck can be fleeting. It may take a long time before you hit the right combination to collect—but *collect you must*, or you will have wasted your money.

3. **Once a machine becomes positive, it remains positive until someone collects the bonus, and then the collection is reset and the positive machine is no longer positive.** Generally, the more you play, the more positive the machine becomes. Can you imagine your frustration if the following happened? You deposit the last $20 you have in your pocket (or purse) into a positive game. You play and play and you don't collect. You play the entire $20 and still don't collect. Grumbling, you get up from the machine and go to your room to get some more money. When you return to the machine, you find that the jackpot has been collected. It is no longer positive. By not having sufficient money in your pocket, you not only lost your chance at the bonus, you blew $20. If you left to get more money before playing, someone else may have still gotten the bonus, but it would have cost you nothing!

4. **You must play until you collect the prize, and if you don't do this then you are purposely giving up your advantage.** Make sure you have enough money with you—in your pocket! This is not like playing a regular slot machine, where you flee once you have started to lose a good portion of whatever your session stake is. Not on these machines. You should have the proper amount of money to assure that you win the game.

5. **Quit playing when you no longer have an advantage.** If you try to build up the symbols, instead of letting the average-slot player build them up, you are just a regular slot player yourself and you then will have no advantage.

6. **Once you collect the bonus, *verify* if you still have an advantage.** There are times when you will continue to have an edge even after collecting a bonus. You should know these times on different machines. If you do not have the edge, then quit playing and move on. Most games lose the advantage once you collect the bonus— most but not all. When you collect, look at the game. Do you still have an advantage? You will have a strong urge to continue playing, but don't unless the machine is still positive.

The above are the six simple rules that you must follow to assure you are playing with an edge and playing properly with that edge. Now let's take a look at many of these advantage-play machines.

S&H Green Stamps
How It Works:
This is probably the most widespread of the advantage slot machines as I write this chapter. As you play, the appearance of a green stamp with a number on the reels adds that number of stamps to a book. The stamps have a multiplier (1X, 2X, 5X) that multiplies the number of stamps that are collected. It takes 1,200 stamps to fill a book. Once a book is filled, you are given the option to continue collecting or to play the bonus games.

What to Look for:
If the game has 600 or more stamps in a book, it is positive. There is one stamp displayed in the book for each 100 stamps collected, so look for six stamps. Six stamps is one row or half a book. The actual number of stamps is also displayed near the books.

How to Play:
Play 25 lines at one credit per line until you play the free games. This amounts to 25¢ a spin for a 1¢ machine, 50¢ a spin for 2¢ machines and $1.25 a spin for 5¢ machines. Once you fill a book (1,200 stamps), you will be given a choice to play free games or to continue filling another book. Play the free games—*do not* continue filling another book.

Bankroll Requirements:
Your minimum bankroll must be *at least* 2,000 credits. This amounts to $20 for a 1¢ game, $40 for a 2¢ game, and $100 for a 5¢ game.

Comments:

Most S&H Green Stamp games have a feature where you can immediately stop the spinning by hitting the spin button. Take advantage of this feature to minimize the time spent playing this game. The faster you play, the better for you. Get your winnings and leave.

This game is fairly volatile. You will tend to have many smaller wins and losses with occasional fairly large wins and losses. Don't let a losing game tempt you to stop play before you collect the free games.

Double Diamond Mine

How It Works:

There are three shafts that hold diamonds. A diamond is added to a shaft when the corresponding reel contains a diamond symbol. When a shaft is filled, you collect the bonus. Once you collect the bonus and the shaft is emptied, reevaluate whether you have an advantage or not.

What to Look for:

This game is positive when any of the following is true.
- One shaft contains nine diamonds
- Two shafts contain eight diamonds each
- Three shafts contain seven diamonds each

How to Play:

Play one credit per spin until you collect the bonus. This amounts to 25¢ a spin for the standard 25¢ machine.

Bankroll Requirements:

Your minimum bankroll must be at least 80 credits. This amounts to $20 for the 25¢ game.

Comments:

This game is not very volatile. Games tend to be fairly short. You will tend to win most games and sometimes for a relatively large amount. Losses tend to be fairly small.

Triple Diamond Mine
How It Works:

Triple Diamond Mine works exactly the same as Double Diamond Mine. There are three shafts that hold diamonds. A diamond is added to a shaft when the corresponding reel contains a diamond symbol. When a shaft is filled, you collect the bonus. Once you collect the bonus and the shaft is emptied, you must reevaluate whether you have an advantage or not.

What to Look for:

This game is positive when any of the following is true.

- One shaft contains nine diamonds
- Two shafts contain eight diamonds each
- Three shafts contain seven diamonds each

How to Play:

Play one credit per spin until you collect the bonus. This amounts to 25¢ a spin for the standard 25¢ machine.

Bankroll Requirements:

Your minimum bankroll must be at least 80 credits. This amounts to $20 for the 25¢ game.

Comments:

This game is not very volatile. Games tend to be fairly short. You will tend to win most games and sometimes for a relatively large amount. Losses tend to be fairly small.

Fishin' for Cash
How It Works:

Fishin' for Cash works exactly the same as Double Diamond Mine and Triple Diamond Mine, except fish are used instead of diamonds. There are three columns that hold fish. A fish is added to a column when the corresponding reel contains a fish symbol. When a column is filled, you collect the bonus. Once you collect the bonus and the column is emptied, you then reevaluate whether you have an advantage or not.

What to Look for:

This game is positive when any of the following is true:

- One column contains nine fish
- Two columns contain eight fish each
- Three columns contain seven fish each

How to Play:

Play one credit per spin until you collect the bonus. This amounts to 25¢ per spin for the standard 25¢ machine.

Bankroll Requirements:

Your minimum bankroll must be at least 80 credits. This amounts to $20 for the 25¢ game.

Comments:

This game is not very volatile. Games tend to be fairly short. You will tend to win most games and sometimes for a relatively large amount. Losses tend to be fairly small.

Wild Cherry Bonus Pie

How It Works:

A Wild Cherry symbol in one of the nine visible reel positions (three rows, three reels) adds a cherry to the corresponding section of the pie. Each section requires six cherries to fill it—54 cherries to fill the entire pie.

When a section of the pie is already full, the cherries are added to the corresponding section of a "bonus" pie. When the main pie is filled, the player collects a random jackpot (25–250 credits) and a bonus equal to the number of cherries in the bonus pie. The bonus pie then replaces the big pie, and the bonus pie is emptied.

What to Look for:

This game is positive when five cherries (or fewer than five cherries) are needed to complete the entire pie. They could be needed in one to five different sections. It is the *total* number of cherries needed that is important.

How to Play:

Play one credit per spin until you collect the bonus. This amounts to 25¢ per spin for the standard 25¢ machine. If there are two or more cherries required in each of the unfilled sections, play two credits per spin, as you will get two cherries when you land on the needed section. Only bet two credits per spin if *each* of the unfilled sections requires two or more cherries to fill them.

Bankroll Requirements:

Your minimum bankroll must be at least 400 credits. This amounts to $100 for the 25¢ game.

Comments:

This game has some volatility. It may take quite some time to fill the pie and collect the bonus. Wins and losses tend to vary considerably. If you follow the rules completely, the game will never be positive after you collect the bonus because at least one section of the new pie will have no cherries in it, therefore requiring six cherries to fill that section. Since the game is not positive until only five cherries are required to fill the pie, *do not* continue playing this game after collecting the bonus.

Wild Cherry Pie

How It Works:

A Wild Cherry symbol in one of the nine visible reel positions (three rows, three reels) adds a cherry to the corresponding section of the pie. Each section requires six cherries to fill it, with 54 cherries to fill the entire pie. When the pie is filled, the player collects a random jackpot. The big pie is then reset.

What to Look for:

This game is positive when 11 cherries (or fewer) are needed to complete the entire pie. They could be needed in from one to nine different sections. It is the *total number* of cherries needed that is important.

How to Play:

Play one credit per spin until you collect the bonus. This amounts to 25¢ per spin for the standard 25¢ machine. If there are two or more cherries required in *each* of the unfilled sections, play two credits per spin, as you will get two cherries when you land on the needed section.

Only bet two credits per spin if all unfilled sections require two or more cherries to fill them. If all unfilled sections of the pie require three or more cherries to be filled, bet three credits per spin.

Bankroll Requirements:

Your minimum bankroll must be at least 400 credits. This amounts to $100 for the 25¢ game.

Comments:

This game has some volatility. It may take quite some time to fill the pie and collect the bonus. Wins and losses tend to vary considerably. Once you collect the bonus, verify whether the game is still positive. Do not continue to play if it is not positive.

Good Times

How It Works:

There are two versions of this game: three credits with 10X multiplier maximum and two credits with 12X multiplier maximum. Three blanks (ghosts) on the pay line with maximum coin-in cause the multiplier line to be increased by one. A Good Times symbol (the X symbol) that lands on the pay line is wild, and if the other symbols on the pay line combine with it to make a winner, the payoff is multiplied by the left column, which can be a 1 through a 10 or a 12, depending on the game.

If two Good Times symbols land on the pay line, both are wild and combine with the remaining symbol for the win. The normal win amount is multiplied by the second column multiplier (which is the square of the first column multiplier). A winning combination with two Good Times symbols pays 1–100 (or 1–144) times the normal amount depending on the multiplier line.

What to Look for:

This game is positive when the multiplier line is 7X/49X or higher. This is true regardless of whether it is a 10X or 12X maximum.

How to Play:

Play the maximum credits per spin (three credits for the 10X and two credits for the 12X) until you collect a win that has a Good Times symbol on the pay line. After you collect your winnings, you must play one more time to reset the multiplier to a random value. Play the maximum credits. If the multiplier is 7X or higher, continue playing, otherwise depart. You no longer have an advantage.

Bankroll Requirements:

Your bankroll should be at least 800 credits. This amounts to $200 for the 25¢ game.

Comments:

This game is quite volatile. It can take a very long time to win the multiplied bonus Once you sit down, plan to stay a while. You will have many small wins with varying losses. But you will occasionally have a very large win (two wild symbols) that puts you way ahead.

Slot Bingo

How It Works:

A special red or green symbol on the pay line randomly selects a bingo number on the red or green card, respectively. A bonus is collected when you complete a winning bingo card. On some machines, one or two jackpot symbols on the pay line when you complete the winning bingo card will multiply the win by three (one symbol) or nine (two symbols).

What to Look for:

This game is positive when either of the two flashboards (red or green) has 50 or more numbers lighted (selected).

How to Play:

Play one credit per spin until you complete a bingo and collect the bonus. This amounts to 25¢ per spin for the standard 25¢ machine.

Bankroll Requirements:

Your minimum bankroll must be at least 240 credits. This amounts to $60 for the 25¢ game.

Comments:

This game has some volatility. Games can stretch out for a while, or they also can move fairly quickly. Win/loss amounts tend to vary quite a bit.

Money Factory
How It Works:

The game displays a money factory that is full of conveyor belts on which sit "minted prizes" containing various amounts of bonus credits. The conveyor belts are divided into units, and a prize is minted on every fifth unit. The conveyor-belt system moves so that the prizes advance toward the end of the system. When a prize reaches the end of the system, the player is awarded that prize's credit amount.

What to Look for:

This game is positive when a bundle of 200 or more is on the conveyor belt.

How to Play:

Play one credit per spin until you collect the bonus. This amounts to 25¢ per spin for the standard 25¢ machine.

Bankroll Requirements:

Your minimum bankroll must be at least 240 credits. This amounts to $60 for the 25¢ game.

Comments:

This game has some volatility. Games can stretch out for a while, or they may move fairly quickly. Win/loss amounts tend to vary quite a bit.

Kool Kat

How It Works:

When a Kool Kat symbol appears on the pay line, the corresponding pile receives an additional hat of various types. Periodically the hat is a crown that lands on the Kat's head. Having a Kool Kat symbol on the pay line while the Kat has the crown wins the number of hats in the corresponding pile as a bonus. The pile is then emptied.

What to Look for:

This game is positive if any of the following is true:

- There is a crown on the Kool Kat's head
- 99 or more hats are in one pile
- 75 or more hats are in each of two piles
- 51 or more hats are in each of three piles

How to Play:

Play one credit per spin until you collect the hats from one of the piles. After collecting, reevaluate whether you still have an advantage and take the appropriate action; stay if you do, leave if you don't.

Bankroll Requirements:

Your minimum bankroll must be at least 160 credits. This amounts to $40 for the 25¢ game.

Comments:

This game has little volatility. Games tend to be fairly short. You tend to win more than you lose, and many wins can be quite substantial when compared to your risk.

X-Factor

What to Look for:

This game is positive when the multiplier is at 6X or higher.

How to Play:

Play the maximum credits per spin until you collect the bonus. This amounts to 75¢ per spin for the standard 25¢ machine.

Bankroll Requirements:

Your minimum bankroll should be at least 400 credits. This amounts to $100 for the 25¢ game.

Comments:

This game has moderate volatility. Games can last quite a while, or they may move fairly quickly. Win and loss amounts vary quite a bit.

Big Bang Piggy Bankin'

How It Works:

When a special symbol appears on the pay line, coins are added to the piggy bank. When three pigs appear on the pay line, the bonus is collected and the piggy bank is emptied.

What to Look for:

This game is positive when there are 40 or more coins in the piggy bank.

How to Play:

Play one credit per spin until you collect the bonus.

Bankroll Requirements:

Your minimum bankroll must be at least 80 credits. This amounts to $20 for the 25¢ game.

Comments:

This game has some volatility. Games could last a while before you collect the bonus.

Racing 7s

How It Works:

When a red, white, or blue 7 appears on the pay line, the 7 of the same color advances on the racetrack. When a 7 reaches the end of the racetrack, the player is awarded the number of credits indicated for that 7.

What to Look for:

This game is positive when any 7 is within four marks of the end.

How to Play:

Play 1 credit per spin until you collect the bonus. Continue playing if another 7 is within four marks of the end.

Bankroll Requirements:

Your minimum bankroll must be at least 80 credits. This amounts to $20 for the 25¢ game.

Comments:

This game has some volatility. Games could last a while before you collect the bonus.

CHAPTER 25

The Bad and Good of Advantage Slot Play

The bad is obvious: you have to search for these advantage-play games, and these games must be in their positive-player mode. Keep in mind that in order for the machine to be positive, some other slot player must play for a considerable time, dumping his money into the machine and then leaving because he's taken a loss of some kind or has some other engagement to go to.

Sadly, during the week, there are not all that many players around to bump up the advantage for you. Playing during the weekends offers more opportunities to find positive machines because there are many more players spread throughout the casino. Unfortunately, there are also more savvy players—just like you—waiting to take over a positive machine too.

So just like a blackjack player looking for the best game or a dice controller looking for the best craps tables to play on, you must set your mind to the fact that there are going to be downtimes when you will be searching and not playing. It's the real price you pay for beating the house at slots. Other players lose their money; you lose some time. Decide which exchange is better for you.

Short Playing Cycle
After spending time finding a positive game, actual play time at a machine is limited. In fact, you are hoping to hit a win right away,

because the longer you play, the better the chance that you will have a losing session at this machine. Just as a regular slot player does, you are spending more and more money to hit those bonuses, and at some point the return for you will not be a positive one. Obviously, you will not win every time you play a slot machine when it is in a positive-player mode.

Just remember, you are going through this effort to win. It is not about having fun playing—it is about having fun winning. As I wrote many years ago, "Winning is the most fun!" And winning on these advantage-play slots is a howl! Still you have to be realistic about the whole enterprise, or you will be just like those dreaming slot players looking to hit the big ones.

Others Seeking the Same Machines

You may have to vie with others to get a machine that has become positive for the player. Be alert when you are searching for machines. Are there others standing nearby observing the same machines? You may have to move quickly to get it when the current player leaves. Or just the opposite, it may be best to just move on. Do not make a scene if some other player beats you to the machine. That will only help eliminate these good games because casinos do not want arguments among their players. It is better to lose one opportunity than all future opportunities. Obviously there will be more players knowing which machines these are simply because they have read this book.

Not Many Opportunities in One Casino

If you are looking for advantage slot play to garner you mega-comps, you are sadly mistaken. There are many things working against this. First, each casino has only a few advantage slot machines. Secondly, those they do have are only positive for a small amount of time. And you only play them for a short time before they go negative. Again, the reason to play advantage slots is to win money. It is not to win comps. Yes, you will get some slot points by putting in your player's card, but your time spent at these machines will be far more limited than the normal losing slot player's time on the machines.

How can you incorporate these advantage machines into your play? When you come down from your room, immediately go to the machines to see what mode they are in. If you are taking a day trip to a casino, then of course go to the one that has these machines—and the more machines the casino has the better for you.

Table-game players should also incorporate these machines into their play. When you are walking through casinos to play craps using a Golden Touch controlled throw or to use Speed Count to play blackjack or going to Pai Gow poker to get the edge there or to find your favorite positive video-poker game, look for advantage slot machines in a positive state as you stroll through the casino. If you find one, play it. If not, move on. Also when you are finished with a table game, check out the advantage machines again. Play those you find in a positive state, otherwise move on.

Will Every Casino in All Casino Venues Have These Machines?

Sadly, many casinos throughout the country will not have these machines on their slot floors. You can be in a casino town where several casinos have the machines and several others don't have them. Even some whole venues might not have any of these machines. As I write this, these advantage-play machines are fairly common throughout the country, albeit with some pockets where they are missing. I would list where they are and where they aren't except for one thing—next year, next month, next week, or tomorrow, where they were, they now aren't; and where they weren't, they now are.

So, you must do a little scouting to find them for yourself. Should you share this information with everyone you know? That's your choice. Just remember, the more people that know of these machines, the more competition you will have playing them.

Some "Guesstimates" on "Possible" Positive Machines

Machines are taken off slot floors every few months, and some of the machines in the previous chapter might not be in the casinos where you play.

However, other machines with the same or similar pay and banking structures might be placed in those very casinos. My assumption is that if these machines have the same or similar pay structures as the ones in the previous chapter, there is a chance—maybe a decent chance—that when they fulfill the positive-mode requirements they may indeed be in a player-advantage state. I can't promise you that they are, but it is a good guesstimate. I am therefore guessing that these machines, even if they never get positive at the "right" moments, will still be better to play than other machines in their particular denominations.

As mentioned in the previous chapter, all potentially positive slot machines must have something that is "banked." This can be almost anything: cherries, bags of money, coins, bonus multiplier, position along a path, and so on. The bank cannot be reset when a new player begins play—it must continue to build until the bonus is collected regardless of who plays the machine. If the "bank" resets with a new player or if the "bonus" is randomly determined, the machine will not become positive at any point in time. It is not a candidate for you to play, so move on.

It is easiest to recognize and correctly play the potentially positive machines that collect things in the bank the same way, with the same quantities and bonuses as the games detailed in the previous chapter. Some examples are Double Diamond Mine and Fishin' for Cash. They both collect items in three columns. Adding the 10th item in a column collects the bonus and resets the column. Armed with this information, if you see a slot machine with three columns to collect things (any things) that pays a 10- or 20-coin bonus when filled with 10 items, you can play it the same way you would Double Diamond Mine or Fishin' for Cash.

I have also seen machines that are arranged and play exactly like Wild Cherry Bonus Pie but with diamonds instead of cherries. These machines might become positive and play exactly like Wild Cherry Bonus Pie. So be on the lookout for known games with new and different looks. It is a decent bet that they could be just like the original game.

But what do you do when you find a totally different machine but one that banks something that continues to build through multiple players?

You know that this machine could become positive at some point, but how can you determine that point?

Without access to that slot machine's PAR sheet, it is impossible to determine the exact point at which a particular machine becomes positive. According to slot expert John Robison of www.casinocitytimes.com, "The PAR sheet, also known as a PC sheet, tells everything there is to know about a slot machine. It tells how the physical and virtual reels are laid out, what the odds are for hitting each of the winning combinations, and the long-term payback for the machine. Manufacturers and casinos guard these sheets very closely, and they are not available to the public."

Obviously the closer to collecting the bonus, the better chance the machine is in a positive state. Most of the machines in the previous chapter become positive at a point where the bank is roughly 10 percent away from collecting the bonus (90 percent filled). While not definitive, it is a good rule of thumb. If you are very risk-averse, wait until the game is 5 percent from collecting the bonus (95 percent filled). If you are more risk-tolerant, you can begin playing a bit farther away from collecting. Keep in mind, the closer the machine is to collecting the bonus, the better chance it is in a positive state.

There are two other criteria that must also be considered—number of coins to play and bankroll required.

Number of Coins to Play:
Generally there is no advantage to playing more than one coin per spin. If, however, multiple coins are required to advance the bank, play multiple coins. If multiple coins played collects more than the number of coins times the bonus, play multiple coins. For example, one times bonus with one coin played, 10 times bonus with three coins played—play three coins. In all other situations, play just one coin per spin.

Bankroll Required:
Bankroll requirements are a little more subjective. As a general rule, a larger bankroll is required when the difference between the lowest bonus and the highest bonus possible is larger. For games such as Double Diamond Mine, the bonus is a constant 10 or 20 credits. A relatively small

bankroll is required—75 to 100 times the amount required for one spin is normally adequate. For games such as Good Times, where the top bonus can be 100 to 144 times the one-coin bonus, a much larger bankroll is required—at least 200 to 300 times the amount required for one spin. When calculating bankroll, it is critical to remember that you must have enough money with you to play the machine until you collect the bonus. How horrible it would be to play for a half hour and run out of money only to have someone else sit down and collect the bonus. The message—when in doubt, bring more money.

There you have it—all the basic information to find and play a potentially positive slot machine. Regardless of exactly what level you decide to begin playing one of these machines—even if it is just over 50 percent of the way to collecting the bonus—you will probably be playing a more player-friendly game than the standard slot machine. By limiting your play to these games you will win more—or at the least, lose less—money.

The Good About Advantage-Play Machines

You are a winner at a game where almost everyone else is a loser. That's enough of the good for me—and it should be for you too.

In Conclusion

Now you know how to make money playing advantage slot machines. Using a little knowledge, you are now in a position to beat the casinos at a game where other casino players usually get trounced—and you can make money consistently from these former one-armed bandits too.

You do have to make sure you have enough money with you to play the game until you collect. I gave you minimum bankrolls to go with each machine, but those are just minimums. I bring more with me, so I don't ever panic when I am playing. True, the comps you acquire from advantage slot play are minimal, or sometimes nonexistent, but we are not playing these machines to get comps or to have the casino personnel like us because we are losers like everyone else.

Yes, you will have losing sessions. Because a machine is positive during your play does not mean you are absolutely guaranteed to win. But it means you will win more than you lose over time. That is really what it is all about, now…isn't it?

Winning is the most fun!

Glossary

401G: A money-market or other savings account that is for a player's gambling bankroll. This money is to be used only for gambling.

Ace Lock: The brand name for high-security locks used on slot machines.

Action: How much you bet over how long a period of time.

Automatic Payout: This comes directly from a machine and not from a slot attendant.

Award Sign: How much for what symbols the machine will pay. This is listed on the face of the machine above the reels or video screen.

Bad Rack: A player who doesn't pay his casino debts.

Bank: A row of slot machines.

Banking Machines: Machines that save up symbols play after play, player after player, until a jackpot is hit, which is then possibly multiplied by the number of symbols in some way.

Bankroll: How much money a player has to gamble with.

Bar: To ban a player from playing a casino game. Also one of the symbols on a slot machine.

Basic Blackjack Strategy: The computer-derived best play of every player hand versus every dealer up card.

Big Bertha: Giant slot machines.

Big Player: A player who bets a lot of money.

Blanks: On slot machines these are either black lines (look like rectangular gum) or spots where there are no symbols whatsoever.

Bust-Out Joint: A casino that cheats the players.

Buy a Pay or Buy a Play Machines: Machines that will open up many more winning lines and symbols with maximum coin. These are the only machines that should be played with full coin.

Cage: The casino cashier.

Cancel Button: Used in video poker, where you can cancel the choices just made.

Carnival Games: Games that were considered sucker games in sideshows and carnivals. Now refers to games such as Let It Ride, Three Card Poker, Caribbean Stud, and other table games. These are all considered bad games when analyzed mathematically.

Carousel: An area usually containing the same type of slot machines usually placed in a circle.

Cashback: A comp where the player gets a certain amount of cash back for his play.

Cash Box: This is the removable box of a slot machine that contains the coins.

Casino Edge: What percent of the money wagered by a player that the casino keeps. This is expressed as a percentage. If the edge is 10 percent, the casino will keep $10 of every $100 wagered over time.

Casino Host: The people who handle the high rollers and the comps for players whom the casinos feel deserve such comps.

Casino Manager: Individual responsible for seeing the games are functioning properly.

Cash-Out Button: The button you hit to receive your money or credit slip.

Certified Machines: Machines that guarantee a certain percentage payback return on every unit in a bank or on some units in a bank.

Change Person: Person who cashes bills and gives change out in the slot aisles. These people are all losing their jobs at a rapid rate as paper machines start to dominate.

Charles Fey: The inventor of the Liberty Bell, considered by most to be the first real slot machine.

Chasing Losses: Increasing one's bets to make up for past losses with larger wins.

Check: A casino chip or coin made specifically for a given casino.

Cherries: A symbol on a slot machine.

Choppy Game: A game that goes back and forth between the player and the casino with no one seemingly ahead.

Cigar: A symbol on a slot machine or a prize given by the cigar-store owner for a player who hit certain winning symbols on the machine. This was a way to circumvent the laws against gambling. The term, "You won a cigar!" comes from this.

Claw Machine: A novelty device that allows a player to use a metal claw to scoop up coins or dump them into a tray.

Clocking: Keeping track of the decisions of a given slot machine. Sometimes called tracking.

Cold Machines: These are slot machines that have not hit many payable symbols in a while.

Community Machines: These are machines and/or games that can be played by many players at once, such as blackjack and roulette.

Comps: Casino gifts of food, rooms, parties, and so forth to reward players for their play.

Credit Line: How much money the casino will lend you to play their games, based on your level of play and on your bank account.

Credit Manager: The individual who decides how much credit a player will receive.

Criss-Cross Machines: A machine that rewards play when the bars are on the diagonal or are coming up on nonpaying lines.

Crossroader: A casino cheat or thief.

Denomination: A machine's lowest bet.

Double Progressives: Machines that have two progressive jackpots, each building separately.

Double-Up Machine: A two-coin multiplier that doubles the size of the payouts for the second coin with a jackpot for that second coin as well.

Due Machines: Mistaken notion that a machine is about to hit because it has been cold for a while.

Electromechanical Slot Machine: One that uses both electrical and mechanical elements. These were used before the computer-oriented chip machines.

Equal-Distribution Machines: These are machines that do not reward playing more than one coin with increased payoffs. One coin could pay $200, two coins could pay $400, and three coins could pay $600. There is no incentive to play more than one coin.

Free Play: A comp where the player gets free spins of the reels for past play.

Fruit Machines: Slots that use fruits as symbols.

Gaffed Slots: Machines that have been rigged to cheat the players.

Ghost: The stop on a slot machine that is blank.

Grifter: A scammer.

Grind Joint: A casino that caters to low rollers.

Gum: Just as with the "cigar" as a reward for winning symbols, many machines used to give gum out as prizes. The store could buy back the gum—which was a cash prize that skirted antigambling laws. The symbols could be rectangular gum blanks.

High Roller: A player who bets large amounts of money.

Hit Frequency: The percentage of time something is returned to the player. Hits are not necessarily wins. A machine that has a hit frequency of 10 percent will return something to the player one out of every 10 spins over time.

Hold: The real amount the casinos take from their games.

Hopper: The payout system of a machine; also sometimes referred to as the tray that collects the coins that fall out.

Hot Machines: These are machines that have been hitting.

Irregularity: A machine that is malfunctioning.

Jackpot: The highest win on a slot machine, name probably based on the poker term "jacks or better" to open a round of betting.

Jackpot Jumpers: Thieves who claim the jackpot you won is actually theirs or who attempt to steal your money once you get it.

Johnson Act: A federal law forbidding the shipment of any gambling devices except to states that have legal gambling. This took effect on January 3, 1951.

Junket: A special trip of gamblers to a given casino, which is paid for by the casino.

Junket Master: The individual in charge of a junket.

Kibitzer: A person not playing a game but commenting on a game. Technique often used by prostitutes to engage prospective clients.

Lemons: Symbols on a slot machine—generally refers to losing symbols.

Liberty Bell: Considered the first real slot machine.

Light-Up Slot Machines: Created by the Jennings Company, these are machines that have lights on them.

Lightning Slot Machines: These give out rapid payouts and have only large winning symbols and few or no small payouts.

Linked-Progressive Machines: Slot machines that are linked to other slots in a given casino or among different casinos with the intention of giving out huge winning jackpots. These machines have increasing jackpots with every coin played until someone hits the prize.

Long Run: The length of time necessary for reality to be close to its theoretical probability. Casinos are in the long run in a very short period of time since they have hundreds of thousands of machines grinding out decisions 24 hours a day.

Loose Machines: A relative term, meaning machines that give more back than other machines.

Mark: A sucker who can be easily tricked. Scammers go after these suckers by promising them the sun, the moon, and loads of money.

Marker: A line of credit given to casino players. The actual marker looks like a check that can be deposited against your checking account.

Martingale: A double-up or increase in one's bet after a loss to gain back the losing money and put the player ahead. This is an extremely dangerous way to play.

Maximum Coin: Whatever the most coin the machine allows a player to play on a given spin or decision.

Maximum Credit: Whatever the most credits the machine allows a player to play on a given spin or decision.

Mechanical Slot Machines: The oldest slot machines run by gears, pulleys, and levers. The pulling of the handle started everything moving inside the machine.

Megabucks and Other Progressives: Giant jackpot producing progressives linked to other machines in more than one casino.

Microprocessor Machines: Today's computerized machines.

Mills Machines: First fruit-symbol machines.

Mints: Symbols on slot machines.

Money Management: The method a player uses to conserve his or her bankroll so he or she doesn't go bust.

Multicoin Machines or Multipliers: Machines that require full coin to win the maximum amount of money.

Multipay Machines: These machines will pay out on more than one line depending on how many coins or credits are played.

Nail: To catch someone cheating, as in, "We nailed him!"

Near-Miss Machines: Usually illegal machines programmed to make the players think they are close to winning because the jackpot symbols keep appearing just above the winning line.

Negative Mode: When a slot machine favors the house it is negative for the players. Just about every slot machine just about all the time.

Odds: The likelihood of an event happening.

One-Armed Bandits: Archaic term that refers to slots since they have handles that can be pulled. These handles were called "arms," and slot machines had "one arm," and they would take people's money, thus they were "bandits."

On the Square: An honest game.

Paper Machines: Machines that do not use coin but strictly credits. When play is finished, players will receive a coupon for the cash value of whatever credits remain on the machine.

Parlay: Betting one's win on the next decision.

Payback Percentage: What percentage of the money played in a machine that the casino will return to the player. If a machine has a 90 percent payback percentage, it will return $90 for every $100 wagered.

Payline: The line that determines the winning and losing decisions.

Payout Meter: The public display of how much has been won or lost on a given spin and overall during a game.

Payout Percentage: What a machine returns in terms of percentages.

PC: The house edge expressed in terms of percentages.

Peaches: Symbols on a slot machine.

Penny Ante: Small stakes game that has its origin in poker.

Player's Card: A plastic card that looks like a credit card that players can put into the machine for the casino to analyze your play and give comps based on your theoretical loss, also called points earned. The more money you play, the more comps you get, and the more your theoretical loss increases.

Positive Mode: Machines that favor the player during certain periods of their programming.

Power of the Pen: The ability of some casino personnel to give out comps.

Premium Players: High rollers.

Producer: A player who can be counted on to lose a lot of money with regularity.

Progressive Machines: Any machine whose jackpot increases with each play.

Push: A tie.

Pushing the House: A term coined by the Captain that describes a player who can get the casino to give him a better game than advertised. In terms of slots, mega-high-rollers can sometimes get a rebate percentage of their overall losses, which will reduce the house edge against them.

Racinos: Race tracks that have slot machines.

Rating: How a casino sees a player's action for comping purposes.

RFB: Room, food, and beverage; a term for getting everything comped by the casino.

Rhythm: The Captain's idea that the 24/7 rhythm of the casinos is not good for players' ability to play rationally. His belief is that a player should stick close to his or her normal daily rhythm.

RNG: The random number generator that determines which symbols will be shown to the player when he hits the play button or pulls the handle.

Ruin: Losing all one's money.

Rush: A quick winning streak or the feeling one gets from hitting a big payout.

Scam: Trick to get a player to part with his or her money.

Scared Money: Playing with money that you can afford to lose.

Session: A given period of time that one is playing.

Shift Boss: Person in charge of the casino during one of its shifts.

Short Odds: Paying less than the true odds of a bet.

Short Run: A small period of playing time.

Slot Arcade: A casino devoted entirely to slots.

Slot Floor: Where the slot machines are located in the casinos.

Slot Mix: Different machines of different denominations spread throughout the slot areas of a casino.

Slug: Phony coin used to cheat a machine.

Stand-Alone Machines: Machines that are not linked and have no progressive jackpots.

Steaming: A player who gets angry with his increasing losses.

Straight Slots: Nonprogressive machines.

Tandem Slot Machines: Two machines that can be played using one handle or play button.

Tapped Out: Losing all of one's money.

Toke: A tip to casino personnel.

The Captain: The greatest gambling genius of all time.

Tight Machines: A relative term; machines that pay back less than other machines.

Tournaments: Slot players on special machines trying to beat other slot players in total credits won. Playing fast is the key to winning slot tournaments.

Trade Stimulator: Slot machines placed in businesses and racetracks to increase profits.

Underground Joint: Illegal casino, often in basements.

Vegas Flu: The term used for people brought to the emergency room in Vegas because they have stayed up too long, have had too much to drink, or are dehydrated and have usually passed out in the casino or in the elevator or in the hallway or in their room.

Vic: A sucker; short for "victim."

Video Slots Machine: A machine that uses video instead of real spinning reels.

Vig: Percent taken out of a bet to give the casino the edge.

Wild Symbol: A symbol that can be used for any other symbol.

Learn the Golden Touch™
from the World's Greatest Dice Controllers

Are you a winner in business—in your chosen job, career, or profession—but a long-term loser at craps? If your answer is yes, it doesn't have to be, because you can learn how to win at craps. Craps *can* be beaten! It isn't easy and not everyone can do it, but then again, not everyone can be successful in business and life. If you are interested in how to win at craps, read on.

There is only one way to beat the game of craps in the long run, and that is through precision dice shooting and perfecting your dice control at the table.

Dice control is a physical skill that can be learned by disciplined players who are willing to practice and perfect the techniques we teach them in our exclusive Golden Touch™ Craps™ dice-control craps seminars. Our teachers are the greatest dice-control specialists in the world, many with books and major publications to their credit, all with years of winning casino experience behind them!

Prominent sports figures, enlightened professionals, and successful businessmen and women take the Golden Touch™ dice-control seminars because you get what you pay for with Golden Touch™:

- Intense one- and two-day craps seminars on the physical elements of controlled shooting: stance and scanning, set, angle, grab, grip, delivery, spin control, and bounce control!
- Hands-on small-group workshops with great coaches who show you how it's done and work side-by-side and step-by-step with you to master the physical elements of dice control.
- Strong tutoring in maintaining mental discipline, focus, centering, and stamina for making your Golden Touch™ last at the craps table no matter what the distractions!
- Betting strategies based on applying sound mathematical principles, rather than superstitions, so that your Golden Touch™ is not tarnished by poor gambling practices!
- How to maintain your edge while random rollers shoot at the table, based on recent breakthrough mathematical research
- How to win the game within the game of casino craps!
- How to assess your edge and optimize your betting strategies to exploit it!

Classes forming now! More info available at www.goldentouchcraps.com
Call us TOLL FREE at 1-866-SET-DICE or 1-800-944-0406

The Golden Touch Dice-Control DVD

Our brand new two-disc GTC DVD is now ready. ***Golden Touch: Beat Craps by Controlling the Dice*** is a superior, professional product in every way. It is two discs of information, and it is loaded with visuals.

There are **more than 200 controlled throws** shown on the DVD from all angles—front, side, back, tabletop—plus landings, bounces, and back-wall hits. There is also excellent *slow-motion footage* so you can actually see how the dice hit the back wall and land. Some shots go right into the camera from head-on.

Watch four of the best dice controllers in the world and watch them unedited: Frank Scoblete, Dominator, Stickman, and Bill Burton. You will see their shots from every angle from start to finish. You will also be given complete statistics of their throws.

There are no edited shots—you'll see actual practice sessions.

The visuals are remarkable. This two-disc DVD set can be used over and over when you are concerned that your form or throw is somewhat off. The two-disc set costs $299 + $6 for shipping and handling and will be sent priority mail.

Call 1-866-SET-DICE to order by credit card or for more information.

Or go to http://www.goldentouchcraps.com/GTCDVD.shtml.